THE PRACTICAL POWER OF SHAMANISM
Heal Your Life, Loves and Losses

MARY L. STOFFEL

Innovative Order, Inc.

Published 2010
Innovative Order, Inc.
Isanti, MN 55040

IBSN 978-0-9844800-1-2

Cover design by Dawn Mathers

Printed in the United States of America by Lightening Source

Forthcoming Books by Mary L. Stoffel

Helping Rescued and Adopted Animals Heal;
Physically, Emotionally, and Spiritually

To Jim, my soul mate and soul support.
Without you this book would still be just an idea

Drumming CD

The purchase of this book entitles you to a free shamanic drumming CD to be used with the journeys and exercises outlined here. To receive your free CD, you can download it from my website at www.humanimal.com/practicalshamanism.

If this is not possible, please contact me at:

Mary Stoffel
29460 Palm St. NW
Isanti, MN 55040-6093
763-444-8146
mlstoffel@innovatord.com

Contents

About the Book, About the Author   ix
Disclaimer   x
Introduction   1

CHAPTER ONE: SHAMANISM . . . 5
Ancient Wisdom Promotes Modern Personal Empowerment   7

CHAPTER TWO: SOLVING PROBLEMS . . . 11
Heal Your Life, Loves and Losses with Shamanic Journeying
   Relationships   12
   Finances   14
   Health   15
   Life Mission   17

CHAPTER THREE: DIRECT REVELATION . . . 19
Get Access to Hidden Information and Spiritual Guidance
   Some of the Ways Spirits Give us Information   22

CHAPTER FOUR: THE ORIGINS OF SHAMANISM . . . 25
The Roots and Evolution of this Ancient Wisdom
   Core Shamanism   27

CHAPTER FIVE: COSMOLOGY OF SHAMANISM . . . 29
Exploring the Three Worlds: the Lower World,
   the Upper World, the Middle World

CHAPTER SIX: THE SHAMANIC JOURNEY . . . 35
Travel to the Spiritual Realm
   Benefits of Journeying   36
   Theta State   37

CHAPTER SEVEN: YOUR UNIQUE WAY
   OF JOURNEYING . . . 41
How you Journey
   Knowing Where You Are   43
   Interpreting Your Journey   44

CHAPTER EIGHT: HELPING SPIRITS . . . 47
Power Animals, Teachers and Nature Spirits
   Power Animals 48
   There are Many Ways to find Your Power Animal 49
   Teachers 50
   Middle World Spirits 51

CHAPTER NINE: POWER ANIMALS . . . 53
*How Your Power Animal is Significant; Physical Characteristics
and Spiritual Aspects*
   List of Power Animals 53
   Dinosaurs 67
   Mythical Animals 67

CHAPTER TEN: HOW TO JOURNEY . . . 69
Preparing to Journey 69
Journeying to the Lower World 71
Journeying to the Upper World 73
Journeying to the Middle World 76
How to Set Yourself Up for Successful Journeying 78

CHAPTER ELEVEN: QUESTIONS ABOUT SHAMANIC
        JOURNEYING & EMPOWERMENT . . . 83
FAQs About Journeying and Empowerment

CHAPTER TWELVE: MY SHAMANIC JOURNAL . . . 91
Practical Exercises; Sample Journeys; Track Your Progress

   Resources 239
   Bibliography 241

About the Book, About the Author

Four years before this book was written I was sitting in my office where I worked for a computer software corporation. I knew that I was going to be laid off. It wasn't a question of if, it was a matter of when, it would happen. The real question was "What then?" In my fifties with a degree that was long out-of-date, my prospects for finding a comparable position with matching salary were slim to none. Worse, I felt that the corporate culture I had existed in for 22 years had destroyed my creativity and innovative spirit. The future looked bleak indeed. Even worse, I felt that the contributions I had made to the company had little meaning in the world we live in. I felt like the business environment had stolen my soul and I was no longer participating in life.

That's when I had the epiphany. I had been studying shamanism for several years as my own spiritual practice. About 5 years before this I actually started a part-time shamanic healing and teaching practice, sharing what I had learned with others who were struggling with problems and issues in their lives. It was time for me to apply the practical aspects of shamanism to my own life and work with my helping spirits to define and chart my own path. And so the odyssey began. I have used the principles and practices in this book to my own advantage. Many of the exercises have revealed information and insights I needed to find my way. By applying the techniques and procedures outlined here, I manifested the severance package I needed, when I needed it, to leave the corporate world behind forever. Even better, I had a new mission, a new commitment to my spiritual path and a new zest for the limitless possibilities before me. You can do this too.

"The old gods are dead or dying and people everywhere are searching, asking: What is the new mythology to be?"

—JOSEPH CAMPBELL

Disclaimer

The exercises and journeys offered in the journal portion of this book are intended to be used for the reader's process of self-healing and personal problem solving. These suggestions chart a path of personal self-discovery and self-empowerment. It is important, however, to act sensibly and responsibly, and to incorporate this program into any protocol prescribed for you by medical and psychological professionals.

INTRODUCTION

My desire to share the healing power of shamanism with others comes from my own personal healing experience. When I married my soul mate and moved from the city to a semi-rural area I ran right into a hunting culture that was foreign to me. Even though I grew up on a farm in southern Minnesota, I rarely saw deer on our property and hunting was not a part of our lifestyle. In the city, while I was aware of its existence, hunting rarely affected me. My husband, however, grew up in the woods and hunting was an integral part of his life. My stepson, who was eleven at the time, wanted nothing more than to follow in his footsteps.

So there I was, an animal communicator and strong empath, trying to make sense of the emotional turmoil that rocked my world every hunting season. I understood all of the logical aspects of hunting. I am not a vegetarian and I totally agreed that it was better for the deer herd to be culled than to have them dying of starvation during a hard winter. But all of that meant nothing when it was excruciatingly painful to feel the dread and terror of the animals. Add to that the fact that the deer is my main power animal! None of the tools I had accumulated through my spiritual quest even fazed the depth of that pain. I tried prayer, meditation, hypnosis, counseling and therapy but nothing worked, and it almost destroyed my marriage.

In desperation I contacted a shamanic practitioner and described the issue. I had heard of shamanic soul retrieval before and it sounded interesting, but I wasn't really 'called' to follow up on it. Suddenly, it became imperative that I seek out this spiritual form of healing. My husband went with me and we ended up having a joint soul retrieval (this is extremely rare). This entire situation was a part of our contract together and it was necessary that we heal together. My stepson's part of the contract was serving as the catalyst that kept pressure on the situation. The soul retrieval was a life-changing experience. I felt a shift for the better in my emotional stability immediately and as I listened to the tape of the session again and again, that shift became stronger and more noticeable in several areas of my life.

I no longer dissolved in tears at the mere thought of hunting. I was able to think rationally about the positive aspects of hunting. And I was even able to admit that most hunters are very ethical and considerate about not wasting any part of the meat or hide. At the same time I noticed a difference in how I reacted to stress at work. I felt more grounded and stable than ever and able to cope with confrontation and deadlines. This was all extremely interesting as I had been searching for answers to behavior patterns for years. I felt like I was finally getting a feel for how to direct and control my life.

After six months of work on integrating the life force that was restored to me during the soul retrieval I reached a point where I didn't know how to go further. I had come as far as I could with this stage. However, I did know that the underlying issue was still not completely resolved. Hunting season was approaching and while I was greatly improved, I could still feel that deep emotional upset. This was what needed to be addressed. Why did I react to this situation on such a gut-wrenching emotional level? And how could I come to terms with it?

So I contacted the shamanic practitioner again and explained that I needed more help. He suggested a course of shamanic counseling, where the practitioner teaches the client how to do a shamanic journey and how to ask the right questions to get at the root of the problem. This involves a series of journeys, going deeper with each one until the client is satisfied that the issue is resolved. I learned how to travel to the Lower World and work with my power animal, the deer. I learned how to travel to the Upper World and received a healing from my Teacher, Jesus Christ. And I learned how to phrase questions to get the answers I sought.

The answers I received changed my entire perspective on hunting. My power animal, the deer, explained it like this. Man has control of the environment. The deer need a certain habitat to survive as a species. Individual animals sacrifice themselves to give man the incentive to continue to protect and preserve the environment for the survival of the species. In the past, the animals sacrificed themselves so that all species could survive, including man. Now, the agreement is that individuals sacrifice themselves so that their own species will survive. This resolved what I had thought was simply a brutal practice into something that made sense for the co-habitation of the two species.

But it didn't address my deep emotional response to the pain and the killing. For that answer I journeyed to my Teacher, Jesus Christ. There are no words to describe the impact and the glory of receiving this personal healing and guidance from Him. As Jesus placed his hand on my head he told me that the reason I reacted so strongly was because I knew how it felt to have someone hurt me intentionally, and I knew how it felt to the animals. And then the pain eased and my passion to help others heal from their pain was born. And I in turn became a shamanic practitioner.

The purpose of this book is to empower others in their personal healing the way I was helped. The answers are there, you just need the way to access them. The guidance and the healing are available to anyone who asks. The compassionate beings of the spirit realm are ready to come to our aid. And we can find our purpose for being here and take control of our path of fulfillment.

As you work your way through the material you will discover the power of the shamanic journey and feel comfortable with the process of seeking guidance and healing. Maybe I'll meet you in non-ordinary reality!

chapter one

SHAMANISM

Shamanism is an ancient method of obtaining information, guidance and healing for solving problems for the individual or community. It is the oldest spiritual practice known to mankind, practiced worldwide for the last 30,000 to 40,000 years. For many, the word "shaman" refers to a spiritual healer, medicine man or spirit doctor capable of accessing secret knowledge and healing powers. Throughout history, shamans have divined information for their community, and served as storytellers, spiritual leaders, counselors and healers. Those in the "shamanic state of consciousness" (SSC) are able to enter into and perceive "non-ordinary reality" (NOR), as defined by Michael Harner in *The Way of the Shaman*, by means of journeying. An important aspect of shamanism is that it provides a very practical means of solving everyday problems. Some define Shaman as "the wounded healer." If you are experiencing or have experienced wounds in your life, you may be on the journey to be a Shaman for yourself and others!

Modern shamanic practice in our western culture co-exists peacefully with urban life, complex technology and mainstream religion. It is a way of connecting with the spirit in all things and honoring our ancient ties to each other and the environment. Basic techniques for seeing and journeying into the spirit world have been quickly learned and adopted by contemporary men and women seeking ways to reconnect with personal helping spirits in the form of animal or human teachers. These techniques illustrate that the core shamanic experience is really simple, timeless, and universal.

Shamanic practitioners address the spiritual aspects of illness on our behalf by working with compassionate, helping spirits to restore balance, harmony, and life-essence vitality. It is their responsibility to alter their state of consciousness and perceive successfully what others do not. One of the distinguishing characteristics of the shamanic practitioner is the ability to move back and forth at will between ordinary reality (OR) and non-ordinary reality (NOR) with discipline and purpose in order to heal and help others. The shaman does a diagnostic journey to consult with the spirits to determine what type of healing is appropriate for the client. It may be a soul retrieval, a soul remembering, a power animal retrieval, shamanic counseling or general spiritual healing. The shaman also travels to non-ordinary reality to obtain information and guidance for problem-solving for individuals and communities.

Ordinary reality is the world we live in day-to-day. We work, we eat and we sleep in ordinary reality and we receive information through the use of our senses of seeing, hearing, touching, tasting and smelling. We also receive intangible information through our intuition, our sense of knowing something not relayed through the five senses. The physical laws of the universe apply in ordinary reality. Objects fall to the ground due to the law of gravity and machines are powered by hydraulic pressure or electricity. We are familiar with the energy of this reality and we have expectations that certain things are true.

Non-ordinary reality is the spirit world separated from ordinary reality by a veil or boundary. It is populated by spirits that can take familiar forms like animal and human teachers, and by nature spirits, elementals and entities that present their own forms to us. The physical laws we are familiar with do not apply in non-ordinary reality. Animals can talk and fly, landscapes may be surrealistic or ethereal, and information may be conveyed in ways outside of the five senses. The shamanic journey provides a way to travel across the boundary separating ordinary reality from non-ordinary reality to gain access to information not available through our five senses. It provides an opportunity to consult with friendly, helping spirits in their world and bring the guidance and problem-solving advice through into our world. The energy of that world is distinctly different from our own and that distinction becomes apparent to the person who practices journeying. The two worlds do not merge or blend together. When you journey you are either here or there and the discipline of journeying helps you recognize where you are.

Shamanic work is very similar to other spiritual methodologies in that intention is everything. You have control of the process of journeying so you determine the spirits that you will be working with. You can make things happen in the journey without 'making it up'. By setting the intention of the journey and asking for specific information or guidance you direct the flow and the energy of the process. The spirits direct how the information is conveyed and what metaphors or symbols are used to tailor the advice specifically for you. Only you can interpret your journey because only you know the meaning of the metaphors or symbols used.

As you gain experience in journeying you will naturally begin to work with a few spirits known as power animals and teachers. You meet these helping spirits by journeying to non-ordinary reality with the intention of finding those spirits that can give you the answers and the healing you seek. You know that these spirits are your power animals and teachers by asking them for signs and information that proves to be correct. As you continue to work with them a relationship of trust is established and you know that you can rely on the information they give you.

Ancient Wisdom Promotes Modern Personal Empowerment

We all have many aspects to us that combine to form the whole person that we present to the world. We are familiar with the physical, mental and emotional parts of our being, but may not be so aware of the spiritual and energetic aspects that complete our persona. When any of these is out of balance or harmony it can affect our lives in unforeseen distressing ways.

Many people in our culture experience varying degrees of chronic depression and illness, addiction, dissociation, post-traumatic stress syndrome, or just plain chronic bad luck. However, few of us would attribute these symptoms to spiritual imbalance or disharmony caused by traumatic or painful events. Left unresolved, this wounding of our life-force or spirit may lead to mental, emotional, and/or physical illness. I know this from personal experience as my introduction to shamanic healing was literally a life-changing event. As my wounded spirit became whole and vibrant my life reflected a sense of increased harmony and general well-being. Life became worth living again. Even better, it became fun and fulfilling, with a renewed sense of purpose and direction.

The wounded spirit can feel overwhelmed by life in general and problems can seem insurmountable. The underlying condition can be a feeling of powerlessness and lack of control. This is reinforced by the seeming inability to change our circumstances, that we cannot influence the events or people that affect our lives.

In ordinary reality, to empower someone is to give them the authority to do something. In shamanic terms, the concept of empowerment is giving an individual the means to access their own spiritual guidance with the aid of compassionate, helping spirits. Whatever it is you seek, whether information, healing, guidance or the development of your own spirituality, the practice of shamanism gives you the power to fulfill that need for yourself. You no longer require an intermediary to tell you what to do or how to interpret the answers you receive. When you are consistent in your shamanic practice and you have established a relationship with your power animal or teacher, you can rely on the guidance you are given. Empowerment also implies the responsibility to act on the information and guidance you are given from the spirits. They are here to help but only you can effect change in your life by taking back your power and applying it. See Exercise #15.

So as you use this workbook the step by step process will help you feel comfortable traveling on your own journeys to promote healing, seek guidance and figure out how to solve your problems. The power of working with your helping spirits will give you more self-awareness and confidence that you have the ability to make the changes required to control the pace and direction of your life. Feel liberated from self-doubt and insecurity as you control not only the technique but the process in mending your spirit and healing your wounds. Experience the renewed sense of peace and harmony in your life as you discover your purpose and explore your spiritual path. This feeling of vibrant well-being will manifest in all areas of your life as you grow to fulfill your destiny. You control the power of the shamanic journey as you search for the answers to your deepest questions about life, love and the pursuit of happiness.

chapter two
SOLVING PROBLEMS

We are living in challenging times; perhaps the most challenging in thousands of years. We can feel overwhelmed by life in general and problems can seem insurmountable. Many are seeking answers through exploration into various spiritual practices that traditionally have offered knowledge and healing from the realms of non-ordinary reality. This spirit realm can provide information not available through purely logical means.

Shamanism has been practiced for thousands of years, and it can be used now to address the practical problems we all face in our daily lives. Problems like not having enough money to pay our bills, much less save for college or retirement. Problems like career decisions, moving or relocating, and personal relationship issues. Major life changes of marriage, starting a family, and dissolving a relationship can cause anyone to question their judgment and feel powerless. And then there are health conditions that can be challenging or incapacitating. These are the types of situations that all of us deal with constantly. With shamanism, we can know that we are not alone; that help and advice are available for the asking and that we can regain the confidence and the power to control our fortunes and our destinies.

Many of us are also confused about our purpose for being here at all. We feel that we are supposed to be doing something but don't have a clue what that is. We may have questions about our spiritual path and can't tell if we are on the right track. How do we know our mission? And how can this ancient spiritual practice really help us find our way?

Let me be clear: shamanism does not take the place of professional help. In fact, it often works best when used in conjunction with modern accepted therapies such as psychotherapy, counseling, hypnotherapy, and medical practice, to name a few. Shamanism adds the spiritual dimension of healing, restoring balance, harmony and a feeling of empowerment. It provides insight and guidance when making decisions or planning a course of action. It helps us see how we are connected and dispels our feelings of isolation.

Here are just a few life situations and issues that can be resolved using the shamanic journeying techniques described in this book:

Relationships

- **Example:** I always seem to attract a certain kind of person into my life that is more negative than positive. How can I figure out this pattern and how can I change it? You can journey to ask for signs that the pattern is starting to repeat again so you can catch it sooner. You can ask how the pattern started in the first place and how to stop it. See Exercises #16, #17.

- **Example:** A new person has come into my life. How do I know if this relationship is one I want to pursue? You can journey to ask what you need to know about this relationship. Is there anything you need to be aware of? How can you proceed safely and confidently? See Exercise #18.

- **Example:** I am getting divorced after several years with the same partner. How can I cope with feelings of fear and insecurity? You can journey to ask a helping spirit such as a power animal or teacher to come to support you and guide you through the process. See Exercise #19.

- **Example:** I have found my soul mate and it's wonderful but his/her family or relatives do not approve of me or the relationship. How can I change the energy around this situation? You cannot change others so you need to approach this as your issue. You can journey to ask what you need to do or change to diffuse the conflict and promote understanding and acceptance. See Exercise #20.

- **Example:** I'm moving to a different state where I don't know anyone. I'm also starting a new job or making a career change. I feel very alone and isolated. How can I quickly start to make new friends and feel more comfortable? You can journey to your power animal or teacher and ask for support during this time. You can also ask for ideas for making connections in the community. See Exercise #21.

- **Example:** I have been in the same relationship for a long time. It feels very comfortable but I don't want to get complacent and start taking things for granted. How can I spice things up a little? You can journey to ask what you need to do or change to inject more excitement into your relationship or to address any long-standing issues between you and your partner. See Exercise #22.

- **Example:** I have recently dissolved a relationship/marriage and bear the emotional scars to prove it. I feel that I am ready to move on now but I cannot let go of the feelings of anger/bitterness/hate/regret, etc. Your helping spirits can help you heal and restore your sense of peace and serenity. See Exercise #23.

- **Example:** I have recently remarried and my partner has children from his/her first marriage. How can I fit into their family and be a GREAT step-parent? You first need to ask your helping spirits for lots of support. Then ask their help in dealing with situations as they arise. See Exercise #24.

- **Example:** I have a physically, emotionally or mentally challenged child. I'm doing the best I can but keep feeling that I could do more. How can I find more resources and time to help my child thrive? In addition to working with conventional means to help your child, through shamanic journeying you also have access to the power and support of the spirit world. See Exercise #25.

- **Example:** My child is experiencing behavioral issues in school and is having trouble with peer relationships. What can I do? I feel so helpless. The power of shamanic journeying can show you ways to help both your child and yourself. See Exercise #26.

- **Example:** I have aging parents and I'm trying to do what's best for them, even when they resist my efforts. How can I respect their wishes, work within the social system, keep them safe and secure, and keep myself sane in the process? Your helping spirits are eager to support and guide you in every way. All you have to do is ask! See Exercise #27.

Finances

- **Example:** I have lost my job and have been unable to find work. I've tried the traditional methods for getting a job but nothing is happening. Where do I go from here? You can journey to find a helping spirit, either a power animal or teacher, who will give you insights on new ways to market yourself. You can even keep journeying to ask "OK, now what is my next step?" See Exercise #28.

- **Example:** I have steady income at this time but it just doesn't go far enough. How can I pay my bills, save for retirement or college, AND still manage to have a life? The spirits can help with resource allocation or by helping you find new sources of income. Journey to ask for information to determine what fits your situation the best. See Exercise #29.

- **Example:** I have been offered a job that would be a new and exciting promotion, but it would require relocation. How can I make an informed decision about whether or not to accept it?

In addition to researching the company and location through conventional means, you can journey to ask if this is a good fit for you and your family. Keep journeying on different aspects of the move, the community, the company and the job until you are satisfied that you are making the right decision. See Exercise #30.

- **Example:** My finances are in dire straits. There are many agencies, companies, and organizations that help people get out of debt and back on track. How do I know which is the best for me and my circumstances? How can I make the best decision on how to proceed? It is important to research each option through conventional means, but there is also an emotional/spiritual aspect to consider. Work with your helping spirits continually to ensure that you are on the right track. See Exercise #31.

- **Example:** I have lost the job I held for many years and that career path is now out-of-date. I must go back to school or get further training to be competitive in the job market. How do I know where to go and what new career to pursue? In addition to using the resources provided for unemployment career counseling, you can journey to your helping spirits to discover what work would make you feel happy, fulfilled and valued. See Exercise #32.

- **Example:** I am thinking of starting my own business. I've done a lot of research but still have fears and reservations about going out on my own. How do I know if this is the right thing to do? Journey, journey, and journey some more to ask for support, help and guidance. See Exercise #33.

Health

- **Example:** I have had a health condition for years that never seems to get any better, no matter what protocol I follow. There may be an emotional or spiritual imbalance affecting this condition that needs to be addressed or brought into harmony. Journey to your helping spirits to ask what issue, memory, belief system or incident is affecting your ability to heal and how you need to resolve it. See Exercise #34.

- **Example:** I suffer from anxiety attacks and depression and have been on medication for both. I feel that I'm missing out on life and would like to find a way to happiness and fulfillment. Can this method help me? The power of shamanic journeying works with and enhances professional therapies, helping you define and cope with the underlying issues. You can ask your helping spirits for support in this difficult time and for practical actions you can do to take back control of your life. See Exercise #35.

- **Example:** I am carrying excess weight, which is affecting my health and self-esteem. I've tried many diets and eating programs but always seem to sabotage any progress I've made. What is causing this and what can I do about it? You can journey to your power animal or teacher to ask what the underlying cause is for the extra weight. What are the practical steps you can take to change your approach to reaching your health goals? See Exercise #36.

- **Example:** I am a healthcare provider and I am very dedicated to giving the best care I can to my patients/clients. But I get tired and burned-out, emotionally drained and spiritually bankrupt. How can I stay in harmony and balance, giving and receiving physically, emotionally and spiritually? In the helping professions you need lots of spiritual support and you can get that through the power of shamanic journeying. The spirits will help you keep your commitment to providing excellent care and show you how to take care of yourself in the process. See Exercise #37.

- **Example:** I (or my spouse) have been diagnosed with a life threatening disease (i.e. Alzheimer's, cancer, heart disease, auto-immune disorder, etc.). How can I learn how to cope physically, mentally, emotionally and spiritually? All of these aspects of the situation can be addressed by journeying and asking the spirits for support and guidance through this difficult time. See Exercise #38.

Life Mission

- **Example:** I have a good family life, adequate income, and work that I enjoy, but something is missing and I don't know what it is. I feel that I'm supposed to be doing something more, contributing in some way, but have no clue how to figure it out. You can journey to your helping spirits to ask for signs that you are on the right path. You can also ask that opportunities to learn about spirituality be made available to you. See Exercise #39.

These are just a few examples of how using the guiding and healing techniques of shamanism can restore balance and harmony to our lives, with peace, serenity and confidence. It re-affirms that we can determine what is best for us and helps us achieve it.

Remember, when you tap into the realm of non-ordinary reality, all answers are available to you when you practice consistently and learn the language of that reality.

chapter three

DIRECT REVELATION

When we struggle with a dilemma or have a problem that needs to be solved, the first thing most of us do is seek information or advice. We look for objective guidance from people that we trust, people that we know we can count on for support. And we gather data that will help us make an informed decision to the best of our ability. When we have done all we can to weigh the facts and the pros and cons, we resort to going with our intuition, our gut feeling. This assumes that we can make a decision at all. Sometimes we are paralyzed by fear or simply cannot see a solution. We feel unable to move forward, at the mercy of forces beyond our control.

When I was incapacitated by my own emotional situation, I tried all of the self-improvement and consciousness raising tools I had studied over many years. I had married my soul mate and moved to a hobby farm in the middle of hunting territory. As an animal communicator and empath, I struggled with emotional turmoil during hunting season, trying to come to terms with a culture that I understood intellectually but could not condone emotionally. My eleven year old stepson passionately wanted to hunt, I was an emotional wreck, and my husband, who had grown up in the woods, was caught in the middle. It became imperative that I find a solution to this issue before it tore our new family apart.

As I worked my way through prayer, meditation, hypnotherapy, counseling and journaling, nothing gave me any insight into the issues involved much less how to address the problem. It wasn't until I found the power of shamanism that I received information I could use and experienced a healing that helped me restore balance and harmony to my life. The shamanic healing technique used was a soul retrieval, performed for me by a professional shamanic practitioner. Soul loss occurs when a person experiences some form of trauma, which can include a near-death experience, loss of a loved one, a severe illness or abuse of any kind. When this happens we lose crucial parts of our life force and vitality, leaving us vulnerable and unable to cope with stressful situations. The soul retrieval healing process finds this lost soul essence in non-ordinary reality and restores it to the person making them whole again. This healing journey restored to me parts of my life force or spiritual essence that I had lost through a prior traumatic experience. This process also restored my strength and resiliency, making me whole again and better able to cope with distressing situations. It took me six months to assimilate and integrate this energy healing, and it helped my overall health and well-being tremendously. But there was still an emotional part of the puzzle that had not been resolved. It wasn't until I learned to journey for myself, to ask my own questions, that I was able to get at the root of the problem.

My power animal is the deer, so it was truly fitting that my questions prompted me to journey to the Lower World so I could ask deer what I needed to know about the situation. Deer spoke to me one-on-one, explaining the ageless agreements around hunting from the prey's point of view, so that I could understand that this was not just exploitation, but a way to preserve the habitat the deer needed to survive. Through direct revelation from the prey animal involved, I had discovered a system that gave me the information and the healing I needed to resolve the issue. It allowed me to chart my own way to peace and serenity at my own pace. It not only helped me solve the initial problem, it brought renewed vigor and hope to my life. If it could make such a difference in my life I knew I could bring this same healing to others. That was the beginning of my life-long shamanic spiritual practice.

Direct revelation refers to the way we get information during the shamanic journey. The journey is a combination of your intention, what you are seeking, and the answers or information conveyed to you by the spirits. This process takes place in their realm, in non-ordinary reality, so they control how the information is relayed to you. With your intention you ask for the answers you need and you go 'face-to-face' or 'one-on-one' with a helping spirit you have worked with and that you trust. The information is given to you directly by that spirit at that time in the journey, a one-on-one exchange. There's no one else there who must intercede for you, no one is channeling the information to you, and no one else can interpret the answer but you. This is the principle of direct revelation. You go directly to the source where the information can be found and you find it in a form only you can understand.

Spirits often convey information in unorthodox ways, using metaphors, symbols and examples. They seldom present the answers in a yes/no black and white straightforward way. Instead, you are expected to figure out the true meaning of the information. In fact, if you only accept the information at face value (literally) and don't look for the deeper connotations, you are missing an opportunity to gain innovative insights into the issue. If you get something you don't understand, you simply go back again and ask for more examples or for clarification. Or you can ask the question in a different way or journey to a different spirit to get another viewpoint. As you work with your helping spirits you get to know how they choose to interact with you and it becomes easier to decipher what they are telling you.

A very powerful way to develop your comfort with understanding the messages you are given is to create a journal and record every journey, your interpretation of it, and then track in your external life how the messages were validated. You are learning what some call The Language of Your Personal Universe. It is an exciting process and builds upon itself. Journaling and studying what your messages might mean will build your confidence in this information and also help you develop your own abilities to interpret what you learn in non-ordinary reality. As the evidence mounts that this process really works, your confidence and self-empowerment also increases. You know that you can trust the information and guidance given to you by your helping spirits.

Some of the Ways the Spirits give us Information

- Teachers and power animals may speak directly. You may actually hear them in the journey. Or you may hear them telepathically in your mind.

- Your helping spirit may accompany you as you travel to the place you are asking about and show you a scene or event taking place. It is up to you to figure out what this scenario has to do with your question.

- Your helping spirit may take you to the void and show you what you are manifesting.

- You may arrive in non-ordinary reality in a landscape that has something to do with your question or intention. The details of the landscape are a part of the answer.

- You may see nothing at all, only darkness, but just 'know' what the answer is.

- You may see colors, hear music, or feel emotions that evoke reactions in you. For example: black smoke, shining crystals, pastoral scenes, pleasant breeze, violent storm, etc. These would have meaning for you that would help you interpret the journey.

I know a fellow shamanic practitioner, a young man, who never saw his power animal or teacher. In fact, it didn't matter which world he journeyed to, he just saw blackness, like the void. So at first he assumed that he wasn't doing it right. Yet when he asked a question in the journey, he always got the information he needed. As he continued to practice and learned to accept what he was getting from all of his senses, he realized that he was receiving an abundance of information and knowledge he could not have accessed on his own.

A student in one of my Introduction to Shamanic Journeying workshops was a graphic artist so she expected to see wondrous things on her journeys. Imagine her dismay when she was met with total blackness in her first journey to the Lower World. She saw no landscape at all. Of course, she was certain that she must be doing it wrong. It wasn't until I stressed the fact that she must pay attention to EVERY sense that she began to recognize the feelings and the sense of 'knowing' that she had experienced. Her power animal was helping her develop her range of interpretation by denying her access to her comfortable way of doing things. By the end of the day, when she had really focused on what she was getting with all of her senses, her power animal finally allowed her to 'see' a landscape through a tiny pinhole.

These are just a few of the ways you might get information. Everything you experience in the journey is important, so you must pay attention. Equally important is that you record immediately what you experienced because you may forget important details. It is important to remember that journeying is a very individual process. I cannot tell you how you should feel in the journey because there is no right way or wrong way to do it. Similarly, I cannot tell you that you will get information in a certain way because everyone does it differently. It makes no sense to compare your journeys with anyone else, because even if we all journey on the same question no two journeys are the same. We may get similar answers in very different ways. What matters is that you get the answers you are seeking. See Exercise #4.

chapter four
THE ORIGINS OF SHAMANISM

The ancient wisdom of shamanism traces its roots back to the Stone Age (technically known as the Paleolithic Age), but is still vibrant and relevant today. Traditional indigenous healers use it around the globe, from Siberia to Australia, from Southeast Asia to North America. The ancient methods have also been put to contemporary, everyday personal use for self-help and self-healing. Shamanism is adaptable, able to remain practical and relevant, as communities have changed from nomadic or agricultural to the modern global societies of today.

Traditionally, healing or spiritual practitioners, called shamans, contacted spirits to work to heal a patient or to obtain wisdom and advice. The shaman entered an altered state of consciousness, the Shamanic State of Consciousness (SSC), where he/she could see deeper truths and gain insights for understanding and healing. After completing the work, the shaman returned to the Ordinary State of Consciousness (OSC). Depending on the culture, the shaman might be an ordinary individual chosen by the spirits to be a healing or spiritual leader, or he/she might be raised as a holy person or priest who is part of a religious system. In many cases the shaman was also the storyteller, the historian and the spiritual teacher of the tribe. The shaman consulted with the spirits to obtain information that the tribe needed to survive, such as the best place to find water, or where the hunters should go to find game. In many cultures shamans would specialize in certain healing or divination practices, some doing only soul retrievals and others helping the deceased to cross to the afterlife. Also depending on the culture, the shaman might use hallucinogenic substances to achieve an altered state of consciousness.

There are many cultural traditions used by shamans to effect healing, incorporating dance, chanting, drumming and rattling, working with sacred symbolic objects, and the use of herbs and medicines. But the essence of shamanism remains the same, namely the ability to enter the world of non-ordinary reality and enlist the aid of compassionate, helping spirits.

Modern shamanism does not conflict with religious beliefs or doctrines. It enhances religious faiths and traditions, which often over the years were integrated with shamanic rituals and ceremonies. Shamanism is more a way of living in an awareness of our connection with all things. It honors life and strives to bring everything into balance and harmony. This is particularly important now with globalization affecting every aspect of life on this planet. We are all learning that change in one area causes change on the other side of the world. We are all connected.

Modern practitioners using shamanic techniques usually don't call themselves shamans. Normally the honorific name of shaman is reserved for traditional practitioners or modern shamans engaged in traditional practices. Recently, a type of modern shamanism has emerged, where individuals use the traditional techniques of drumming, dancing and chanting to enter the Shamanic State of Consciousness (SSC) for healing and personal growth. This is an altered state of consciousness that allows the person to travel or journey to non-ordinary reality to commune with the spirits for help with self-empowerment and self-healing. You, too, can use the power of the shamanic journey to obtain information and guidance to re-gain control of your life.

Core Shamanism

In the beginning, shamanism was practiced by tribal communities who tended to stay in specific geographic areas. These communities were very in tune with their environments, dependent on the animals and plants of the area for survival. Their beliefs, rituals and ceremonies reflected this intimate knowledge and developed into what we call cultural-specific shamanism. Even though the underlying essence of shamanism was the same, it was expressed in culturally specific ways. The shamans of Siberia did essentially the same healings and divinations as the shamans of the Amazonian rain forest, but they did them in different ways because their environments were so different.

Michael Harner, anthropologist at the University of California, Berkeley, and founder of the non-profit Foundation for Shamanic Studies, was the first to define the concept of core shamanism. Harner found in his studies of shamanism as it was practiced worldwide, that all of the indigenous shamans were doing basically the same things, just in culturally specific ways. Starting in the 1970's, Harner was the first to train contemporary Westerners in the practice of the classic ways of shamanic healing, in the form of what he called 'core shamanism', meaning that he taught just the basic techniques without using or 'borrowing' cultural rituals or ceremonies.

Trained by the Foundation for Shamanic Studies, many modern shamanic practitioners in North America and Europe apply these basic techniques of shamanism for their own personal development and self-healing, help clients who come to them for healing, and teach self-empowerment and self-healing to others.

chapter five

COSMOLOGY OF SHAMANISM

Exploring the universe of shamanism differs depending on whether you are studying indigenous, cultural or core shamanism. Different cultures define non-ordinary reality in various ways and with culturally specific names. Most cultural forms of shamanism describe going to different areas of non-ordinary reality to perform different functions. The shaman may search for answers in the Sky or Upper World. He/she may retrieve a guardian power animal for a patient or client from the Lower World or Underworld. Core shamanism, as practiced in North America, describes the geography of non-ordinary reality in terms defined by Michael Harner, founder of the non-profit Foundation for Shamanic Studies. There are three worlds in core shamanism: the Upper World, the Middle World and the Lower World. These worlds do NOT equate to Heaven, Earth and Hell as defined in the doctrines of many religions.

The energy of the Lower World feels grounded and earthy. The landscape tends to be much like our reality, with mountains, jungles, plains and forests. By contrast, the Upper World feels more ethereal, more spiritual. The landscape reflects this with crystal palaces, pastel or muted colors or sometimes complete darkness. The energy of the Middle World is most like ordinary reality as the veil between the worlds is quite thin here. The landscape also is most like our normal world.

The shamanic practitioner has spirits in all three worlds that help with healing, guidance and information. Each world has resident spirits that perform various functions and the shamanic practitioner goes to the spirit he/she needs to work with, where ever they may be. The spirits that help a shamanic practitioner may change depending on the need, but it is important that the practitioner establish a good working relationship with them so he/she can trust the information received.

When you are searching for information, guidance or healing, the world you go to is not as important as the spirit who will help you. The Upper World is not more powerful than the Lower World and power animals are not more powerful than teachers. It IS important that you establish a good working relationship with your helping spirits and you do that by journeying to them often. As you become familiar with collaborating with them, you know that you can trust the guidance that they give you. Sometimes a compassionate spirit will appear to help you with a particular problem or issue and then leave when their job is done. However, you can always ask them to stay. See Chapter Eight for more information on identifying and working with your helping spirits.

The Lower World is often the easiest to visit when getting started in journeying. It is the place where you go to meet your power animal(s) and the landscape can be very similar to ordinary reality. See Chapter Nine on power animals for descriptions and characteristics, as well as the spiritual significance of several animals that may volunteer to help you. Actually, power animals can and do go anywhere in non-ordinary reality and the landscape in the Lower World can be anything your helping spirits choose to show you. When traveling to the Lower World, there should be a sense of going down to start the journey and a sense of coming back up when returning to full awareness. This transitional phase of the journey often appears as a tunnel with one end in ordinary reality and the other end in non-ordinary reality. As you traverse the tunnel you move between realities.

The portal or entry point to the Lower World is often a feature of nature that you are very familiar with so it is easily pictured and recognized. This can be a cave that you know well, a favorite tree, or a body of water, such as a pond, lake, stream or waterfall. It is important that you are comfortable with your portal and that you can visualize it clearly. For example, choosing a lake that you must dive into will not work well if you don't know how to swim in ordinary reality. See Exercise #2.

My entry portal to the Lower World is a place I know well from my childhood. I grew up on a farm in southern Minnesota and there was a bayou in our pasture. One end of the bayou was very mucky and some said there was actually quicksand there. As children, we were warned away from that area, but as a shamanic practitioner it became the perfect place for my tunnel to the Lower World. As I start my journey, I picture myself approaching that end of the bayou. I can see the water over the area I always associated with quicksand. I dive into the bayou, into the quicksand, which propels me down into a tunnel that magically appears as my route to the Lower World. This portal worked beautifully for me the first time I journeyed to the Lower World and I have used it ever since. I have always felt very safe and comfortable both going to the Lower World and returning to ordinary reality.

Going to the Upper World involves using a feature of nature to go up rather than down, but without the use of a tunnel. For example, you can use a tornado to lift you up, you can climb a tree or walk a path up the side of a mountain. Since a tunnel is not available to serve as the transition between realities, there must be some form of boundary to mark the entry into the Upper World. This often takes the form of a layer of cloud or fog that you pass through. Entry into the Upper World is experienced as a change in landscape or a distinct difference in energy. If you have not passed through the boundary, you can travel deeply into outer space and still be in ordinary reality. The energy of the Upper World is often described as being more ephemeral. The colors may be softer, with more pastels, and the landscape may contain ice palaces and crystal structures. Helping spirits known as teachers are found in the Upper World, but like power animals they can go anywhere in non-ordinary reality.

I currently live on a hobby farm in Minnesota. Between the house and the horse barn stand two eighty-foot tall cottonwood trees. To reach the Upper World, I climb up one of these trees. The first time I did this, I reached the top of the tree only to realize that I had not crossed through any boundary. I was still in ordinary reality and had run out of tree. Just at that moment in my journey, a sunbeam broke through the clouds and presented itself as a tangible means for going up further. I grabbed the sunbeam and rode it up through the cloud layer that was the boundary between the worlds. I had entered the Upper World and have used this route ever since. When I return to ordinary reality, I ride the sunbeam back down to my tree and climb down to the ground.

The first time I journeyed to the Upper World I went through the cloud layer and was surprised at what I found. If you have ever flown in an airplane above the cloud layer you know that it looks like you could get out of the plane and walk on the clouds. That was what I saw after passing through the first cloud layer. I looked up and there was another cloud layer so I rode my sunbeam up through that one too. I could see what looked like shapes off in the distance but nothing recognizable and nothing in the immediate vicinity. It wasn't until I went through the third cloud layer that I finally found my Teacher. That was how I found that the Upper World has levels. When I mentioned this to other shamanic practitioners I found that the Lower World also has levels. All of them have unique characteristics that can be explored with your power animal(s) and teacher(s). See Exercise #5.

The Middle World is the most like the world we live in, being the spiritual dimension of this reality. Here we meet the nature spirits, the divas, the spirits of the plants and of the land. Entry into the Middle World also involves crossing a boundary or transition point, such as a bridge, or passing through a copse of trees, or entering a garden through a gate. There must be an easily recognized point where the energy shifts and you enter the spirit world. Helping spirits in the Middle World might be trees, plants, fairies, elementals or divas. A good journey to try in the Middle World is to get to know the spirit of the place where you live. What is its history, its likes and dislikes, and how can you live in harmony with it? See Exercise #8.

When I journey to the Middle World, I go through the archway between my two tall cottonwood trees. As I pass between the trees, I can feel the energy change from ordinary reality to non-ordinary reality. The landscape doesn't change but the feeling of the energy certainly does.

Generally, it is best to practice journeying by becoming familiar with the Lower World and establishing a good working relationship with your power animal(s) first. When you are comfortable in this realm you can start going to the Upper World to work with your teacher(s). This will give you a good sense of knowing where you are in non-ordinary reality. After you have experienced the different energies of these worlds you can go to the Middle World to find your helping spirit(s) there. This is the recommended process, but not the only way to proceed.

Some people feel very comfortable in the Lower World and tend to work most closely with their power animal(s). Others are drawn to the Upper World and find it much easier to go up rather than down. Follow the path that works best for you, especially when first starting to journey. The important thing is to gain experience at journeying so you can trust the process and explore the wealth of the information available to you. You can also journey just to explore the other worlds but be sure to go with a power animal or teacher as they serve as our guides in non-ordinary reality.

chapter six
THE SHAMANIC JOURNEY

Central to the ancient system of healing called shamanism is the shamanic journey. Worldwide, shamans in indigenous cultures have used the technique of journeying to access information and healing for the members of their tribes. Although different methods are used to perform the shamanic journey, the concept is the same across cultures. This is a technique to travel to the spirit world, using percussion, chanting, rattling or some form of repetitive beat, to ask for guidance or healing. In some areas hallucinogenic drugs, other substances or deprivation techniques are used to trigger an altered state of consciousness.

Anyone can use the technique of shamanic journeying for day-to-day problem solving, decision-making, getting to know and working with your helping spirits, and self development and healing. This technique can be used to explore your own personal spirituality and expand your awareness and intuition. You will experience a deeper connection to nature, the animals and your environment. Through connecting to the spirit in all things you can discover your purpose and mission in this lifetime. However, for deep emotional and psychological healing, please work with a trained shamanic practitioner who can guide you in the process.

Benefits of Journeying

Shamanic journeying in and of itself is a fun and enlightening experience. It allows access to other worlds and realities, to knowledge previously hidden and to insights previously unattainable. It is possible to get personal answers from helping spirits through direct revelation. The journeyer interacts directly with spirits to gain information, guidance and power to address the spiritual aspects of illness. It is extremely empowering to be so proactive in one's own healing and development. Some of the situations that can be addressed through journeying include:

- **Problem-solving:** You want to ask a question about a problem in your own life which you have not been able to resolve through conventional methods. This may involve a career or relationship situation that you find distressing or a decision that must be made.

- **Guidance:** You are contemplating a lifestyle change and need to consider aspects you may not have thought of.

- **Personal Growth:** You want to determine your mission in this lifetime and ask for confirmation that you are on the right path.

- **Healing:** You feel powerless and out of balance and want to re-establish control and harmony.

- **Contacting Your Spiritual Helpers:** You want to maintain a relationship with your power animals and teachers so that you can trust the information you receive from them.

While shamanic journeying is a powerful tool for personal use, *it is not appropriate to ask for information about or for someone else without their permission.* Always phrase the question or situation from your personal point of view, asking what you need to know or change.

Theta State

Core shamanism teaches that mind altering substances are not necessary to attain the benefits of journeying. By simply using a drum or a rattle you can use a repetitive beat that calms the mind and helps you expand your awareness. In his book, "The Way of the Shaman" (Harper; San Francisco; 1990), Michael Harner, founder of the Foundation for Shamanic Studies, explored the scientific effects of drumming. According to Harner, this repetitive beat when used by native peoples to achieve an altered state of consciousness, closely matches the base resonant frequency of the earth.

Studies have shown that vibrations from rhythmic sounds have a profound effect on brain activity. In shamanic traditions, drums were used in periodic rhythm to aid the shaman in traveling to other realms of reality. The vibrations from this constant rhythm affect the brain in a very specific manner, allowing the shaman to achieve an altered state of mind and journey out of his or her body.

Brain pattern studies conducted by researcher Melinda Maxfield into the (SSC) Shamanic State of Consciousness found that the steady rhythmic beat of the drum struck four and one half times per second was the key to transporting a shaman into the deepest part of his shamanic state of consciousness. It is no coincidence that 4.5 beats, or cycles per second corresponds to the trance like state of theta brain wave activity. In direct correlation, we see similar effects brought on by the constant and rhythmic drone of Tibetan Buddhist chants, which transport the monks and even other listeners into realms of blissful meditation.

There are frequencies/rhythms which when dominant in the brain correlate with a specific state of mind. There are generally 4 groupings of brain waves:

1. **Beta waves** range between 13–40 HZ. The beta state is associated with peak concentration, heightened alertness and visual acuity.

2. **Alpha waves** range between 7–12 HZ. This is a place of deep relaxation, but not quite meditation. In Alpha, we begin to

access the wealth of creativity that lies just below our conscious awareness—it is the gateway, the entry point that leads into deeper states of consciousness. Alpha is also the home of the window frequency known as the Schumann Resonance, which is the resonant frequency of the earth's electromagnetic field.

3. **Theta waves** range between 4–7 HZ. It is known as the twilight state which we normally only experience fleetingly as we rise up out of the depths of delta upon waking, or drifting off to sleep. In theta we are in a waking dream, vivid imagery flashes before the mind's eye and we are receptive to information beyond our normal conscious awareness. During the Theta state many find they are capable of comprehending advanced concepts and relationships that become incomprehensible when returning to Alpha or Beta states. Theta has also been identified as the gateway to learning and memory. Theta meditation increases creativity, enhances learning, reduces stress and awakens intuition and other extrasensory perception skills.

4. **Delta waves** range between 0–4 HZ. Delta is associated with deep sleep. In addition, certain frequencies in the delta range trigger the release of Growth Hormone beneficial for healing and regeneration. This is why sleep, deep restorative sleep is so essential to the healing process.

Modern shamanic practitioners usually achieve the theta state through drumming or rattling. As with all enlightenment techniques, the more you practice the easier it is to enter an altered state of consciousness. The goal is to relax the body and mind, yet stay awake and focused on the intention of the journey. Each journey is undertaken with a specific purpose or intention, even if that intention is just exploration of the spiritual realm.

While you can drum for yourself when journeying, it is easiest is start with a drumming tape or CD. A drumming CD suitable for journeying does not contain any other music, speaking, or variety of beats. Journeying CDs usually have 2–3 tracks with different time lengths of repetitive drumming to accommodate journeys lasting 10 minutes, 20 minutes or 30 minutes. It is unusual and often not necessary to journey more than 30 minutes at a time. Keep in mind that it is difficult to maintain both relaxation and focus for that length of time.

An important feature of the drumming CD is the return or recall beat. This series of beats interrupts the rhythm of the repetitive beat as a signal that it is time to end the journey and return to normal conscious awareness.

A successful journey follows a disciplined format that is simple and consistent. It starts with a path or entry to the spirit world where you meet your power animal or teacher. The question is asked or the intention of the journey is stated and the spirits determine how the information is presented. The journey continues until the recall beat sounds and the journeyer returns to conscious awareness. It is a good idea to record your impressions immediately before they are forgotten.

chapter seven

YOUR UNIQUE WAY
OF JOURNEYING

Most people are plagued by doubts when first starting to journey. Am I doing this right? How do I know? Am I really getting what the spirits are telling me or am I just making this all up? The best thing to do is to keep going and keep practicing. The more you journey the more familiar you become with how to work with your helping spirits.

It is important to note that everyone develops their own way of journeying based on how they perceive the information presented by the spirits. All of the senses are used by the spirits to relay information so do not rely solely on what you 'see' in your journey. Pay attention to anything you hear, smell or taste as well. You may also just 'know' what is happening, even if you don't have visual imagery to tell how you know. All senses contribute to the richness of the journey and to the message that the spirits are sending. A whiff of salty air may signify the vastness of the ocean to one person, while another person may connect with family outings to the seashore. Each person receives imagery and symbols tailored to how they process information.

This is why no one else can interpret your journey for you. The spirits seldom give us definitive answers to our questions. Instead you are given metaphors, symbols and hints that only you can relate to in answering your question. Also, if you just pay attention to the literal sense of the information received, you may miss any under-lying meanings that may tell you what you really wanted to know. Using the example of the salty air in the journey, just making the connection to the family outings is the surface interpretation. Delv-ing deeper into the symbolism may illustrate family relationships that can help resolve current issues or problems.

The general rule is to keep it simple when you journey. *Ask only one question per journey and phrase that question to get the most informa-tion you can on the subject.* You can delve deeper into the question as the journey proceeds as long as you don't switch to a completely new topic. So your question should be open-ended, i.e. "What can you tell me about ...?" or "What can I do to change this situation?"

Asking a yes or no question will only get you a yes or no answer and it may not give you enough information to make an informed decision. For example, let's say that a woman meets a man and wants to know if this will be a good relationship for her to pursue. In her journey she asks this as a yes or no question and her helping spir-its come back with a yes answer. The relationship develops into an abusive situation and the woman learns the hard way to develop her own personal power, integrity and strength. Eventually she comes out of the relationship stronger, more confident and more powerful. In the end, yes, this was a good relationship for her personal growth, but she may have accomplished the same result in an easier way. A better way to ask the question would have been, "What do I need to know about pursuing a relationship with this man?" Then the an-swer could have shown her that while it might be good for her in the long term, getting to that point could be quite painful.

While in the relationship it would be tempting to ask the spirits how to get the man to change his behavior. Since you cannot jour-ney for someone else without their permission, the best way to ad-dress it is to ask, "What do I need to do to change this relationship or this situation?" Then, of course, after asking the spirits for advice its best to follow through with the action they suggest. In other words, only ask the questions that you really want answers to.

As for how you can tell that you are not making this up, the day comes in a journey when you see, hear, smell, taste or just 'know' something that really surprises you. You get an insight or the answer to a mystery that you did not expect. But on reflection you realize that it is exactly the answer you were seeking all along. This is when you truly start to trust that this process really works! In some ways, shamanic journeying is another way to access our own inner wisdom. We already have within us the knowledge we are searching for and the spirits present it to us in ways we can relate to and understand.

Knowing Where You Are

In a shamanic journey we travel from Ordinary Reality to Non-Ordinary Reality. The world we live in, work in, play in and otherwise function in is ordinary reality. It is the world we are familiar with. We know how things work in this world. The laws of physics and gravity apply here. We trust the information we receive through our senses.

In non-ordinary reality there are no rules. Anything is possible. Animals can talk and fly. We can speak to people who have died and work with famous people as our Teachers. We can receive previously hidden information through paranormal senses. Healing can happen with intention and we can learn what we need to know from the spirits through direct revelation.

While journeying it is important to know which world you are in. You are either here or there. That is why there is a discipline to shamanic journeying. You start in ordinary reality. You travel a definite path to a portal or boundary that you pass through to enter non-ordinary reality. You fulfill the intention of the journey, whether it is to gain knowledge, ask for healing or solve a problem. And you return to ordinary reality by the same path. Once your route has been established you use it consistently to obtain trustworthy results. Listening to a drumming tape or CD helps you maintain the theta brain wave state so it is easier to focus and concentrate on the intention of the journey. Never listen to a shamanic drumming CD or anything else that induces the theta state while driving your car or performing any function that requires full awareness.

The shamanic journey is not a trance-like state. It is more like being in a deep meditation where you control going to and coming back from non-ordinary reality. Even if you are interrupted in the middle of the journey you can come back to full awareness, take care of the interruption, and return to the journey simply by restarting the drumming CD and repeating the intention of the journey. As you become familiar with your path going and coming it is easy to feel the energy difference between the two realities.

Interpreting Your Journeys

When first learning to journey, everyone has trouble with interpretation. We need information and guidance and we want it to be given to us clearly and without ambivalence. We'd really prefer to be told what to do, and how and when to do it. Fortunately, our helping spirits know that we also need to reach our own conclusions, based on facts, insights, intuition and revelations. And, sometimes we just know the right answer, even if we can't state the logical reasons for why we know it.

The first rule of interpretation is that only you can interpret your journeys. This is because we all journey in our own unique way. Some people see very clear pictures in their minds, while others actually hear their helping spirits talking to them (you might not want to tell that to a psychiatrist). Other people feel the energy of the spirits and just know what information they are receiving, without knowing how they know it. I have had students who never 'see' anything at all, or who just see colors. I 'feel' what is happening in my journeys and just know what is being given to me. This is why I tell my students to be aware of every sense when they journey. Everything you see, hear, touch, taste, smell or feel is important and provides part of the answer you are seeking.

The second rule of interpretation is that the spirits don't give us black/white, yes/no answers. They present the information in the form of metaphors and symbols, in scenarios and pictures, in examples and feelings. They give us answers with clues that we relate to, that remind us of something, or that we make connections with. Sometimes it's like putting a puzzle together, getting the pieces in the right place to form a picture. Often there are several layers to the information we receive and you can go as deep into the question as you like by asking for more clarification. If you stop at the first level or layer, you may miss additional information that is available. That is why I recommend staying in the journey until the recall beat sounds, asking for more examples that illustrate the various aspects of the issue or question. Your purpose or intention for the journey is to get information or guidance that will help you make an informed decision, and you can keep asking until you are satisfied that you truly understand all of the options available to you. You can also journey to your power animal and your teacher for different perspectives on the same question. Remember that the answer may change depending on WHEN you ask the question. Sometimes the timing simply isn't right for you to act yet, or you need to perform prior steps first to prepare for definitive action.

The third rule of interpretation is that the answer to one question invariably leads to more questions. If they all relate to the same question or topic you can continue to ask them in the same journey, as all you are doing is seeking clarification on the issue. If they start to go off on a tangent it is better to finish this journey and then take the time to think about and define your question for the next journey. That way you are sure that all of the information in this journey relates to your original question and you don't get confused. The basic rule is: one question or topic for one journey.

Finally, if you don't really want to know the answer or if you don't plan to act on the information given to you, then don't ask the question in the first place. The spirits will give you true information even if it is not what you want to hear. If you go to the spirits for counsel and advice, but then consistently decline to follow it or act on it, eventually your helping spirits will become frustrated and impatient with you. So, the best way to approach difficult situations is to explain to your helping spirits that you are looking for options, but you may not be ready to act upon them yet. In fact, you may ask them for suggestions on how to prepare yourself for action in the future. Sometimes issues or problems need to be broken down into steps so they aren't too overwhelming. The spirits can help you do this so that you can develop a plan of action addressing what you can now, and leave the rest for later.

The most important thing to remember is that you have support available to you from the spiritual realm. Our power animals and teachers want to help us succeed and grow and achieve balance and happiness. As we live in harmony and cooperation with our environment and all things, our conscious development affects the whole of creation. As we thrive, so does our world and our universe. In shamanic terms, it is expressed as 'As above, so below; As within, so without.'

chapter eight
HELPING SPIRITS

Shamanism uses the concept of direct revelation which allows us to communicate one-on-one with our helping spirits. We find compassionate spirits willing to help us by journeying to non-ordinary reality with the intention of meeting them and identifying them. The intention of the journey sets the purpose of meeting a helping spirit and they let us know by some means that they are the one we are seeking. The spirit may be in the form of an animal, a mythical creature such as a unicorn, a nature spirit or a human figure. In the journey the spirit may speak to us, use body language or use some other means to connect with us. Once we know who our helping spirits are, we can establish a working relationship with them so that we can trust the information they give us. The spirits volunteer to help us and serve as our guides and guardians in non-ordinary reality. In return we serve as their partners and collaborators in ordinary reality. Our ancestors lived with and honored this connection to the spirit in all things. As humans began to congregate in cities and use machines we lost contact with the natural rhythms and cycles of the physical world.

Try to manage your expectations of how you think your helping spirits will interact with you. It is tempting to think we are doing something wrong if our power animals and teachers don't 'talk' to us or show us exactly the answer to our question. Remember that the spirits often give us information in the form of metaphors or symbols and it is up to us to figure out what they mean. And it is always possible to ask the same question in different ways to both a power animal and a teacher to get different viewpoints. If the information you receive is difficult to interpret, don't automatically assume it is your fault. Simply ask for more clarification or for more examples until you can say "OK, I get it!"

One of my students was very frustrated when he journeyed because all he ever saw was colors that swirled and changed throughout the journey, no matter what the intention of the journey was. His power animal was a parrot with vibrant plumage and a bit of an attitude. When the student began to associate feelings with the colors, he was finally able to 'crack the code' of how this spirit was portraying information. As the student kept asking for more information on what the colors meant in the context of the question being asked, he got more empathic feelings about the situation that could be interpreted as the answer. He was then able to confirm with the spirit that this was indeed the answer he was meant to receive.

Power Animals

Our connection with our power animal(s) helps restore the understanding and appreciation of nature that many of us have lost. You may have had a special affinity for a particular type of animal all your life. The dog, the cat, the horse or another animal may have fascinated you since childhood. So you might expect this special animal to be your power animal or helping animal spirit. However, for shamanic practice this may not be the case, at least not in the way you expect. Since power animals represent our connection with nature, they are usually not domesticated animals. If the horse is your power animal, it is the wild horse of the plains that volunteers to help you.

Power here means spiritual power that comes from inherent knowledge, information or wisdom that the power animal willingly shares with you because there is some mutual need or compatibility between you. This reflects a worldwide belief that the spirits, including animal and nature spirits, need us as companions too and befriend us to exchange support and help. So, while your favorite animal may in fact be your power animal, you must open your mind and heart and allow the spirits to decide which power animal is most appropriate for you at this time. See Exercise #3.

You may have more than one power animal and it is your responsibility to maintain the connection and relationship you have with all of them. You don't have to journey to connect with your power animals. You can call on them anytime in ordinary reality as well. For example, people often ask their power animals to accompany them while traveling. It's like having several guardian angels along.

Each power animal represents the strengths and characteristics of that particular species, so even though you work with an individual wolf, for example, that wolf brings you the gifts and powers of all wolves. Sometimes power animals will give you the name they would like to be called, but others will not. Always ask your power animal how they would prefer to work with you. As you gain experience at journeying, you will also become more comfortable with the personalities and quirks of your power animals.

Power animals are normally found in the Lower World, but they can go anywhere in non-ordinary reality. When first starting to journey it's a good idea to invite them along anywhere you go in non-ordinary reality so you can ask them about unexpected situations.

There are Many ways to find Your Power Animal

1. You can do a Vision Quest. There are many reputable shamanic training programs that offer this method. Do your homework to determine if this is right for you as it may involve fasting and/or sleep deprivation.

2. Dreaming for a power animal is setting your intention to have your helping spirit come to you in a dream. You can then validate this with a follow-up shamanic journey.

3. Dancing for a power animal is asking for the spirit to come to you as an expression of physical movement.

4. You can do an exploratory journey to the Lower World with the intention of meeting your power animal. See Exercise #3.

5. You can have a power animal retrieval done for you by a professional shamanic practitioner.

In a very practical way, power animals serve as our entry into non-ordinary reality. In a spiritual sense our collaborative relationship with them goes far beyond just getting information. It is very self empowering to know that we have these strong spirit helpers volunteering to give us guidance and support. We can trust them to protect us in areas where we are vulnerable and with their help we can develop to our fullest potential. See Exercise #4.

Teachers

Just as power animals reside primarily in the Lower World, teachers are usually found in the Upper World. However, you can journey to the Upper World with your power animal if you wish and your teacher can take you anywhere in non-ordinary reality. While it is not necessary to find a teacher, often one will appear to help you answer a particular question. You may then establish a relationship with this teacher just as you did with your power animal.

In the Upper World you may meet a variety of teachers in human form. Do not be surprised if you encounter religious figures such as Jesus, Mary or Buddha, inspirational figures such as Einstein, or gods and goddesses such as Thor, Athena and Hermes. Many people report having a deceased relative, such as a grandmother or grandfather, as a teacher. It is important that you remain open to the many forms teachers may present themselves in. Your teacher does not have to be a famous or recognizable person. You may find that your teacher is a Native American shaman, a wise elder (either male or female), an ethereal figure such as an angel, or a mythical creature such as a dragon or wizard. See Exercise #6.

Just as with power animals, you can have more than one teacher. As you gain experience in doing your shamanic practice, you may find that your teachers will specialize in certain areas of information or tasks. Again, it is your responsibility to maintain the relationship with all of your teachers by working with them on a regular basis. Trust comes with familiarity and experience, so the more you practice, the better you are at interpreting what you get. See Exercise #7.

Middle World Spirits

The spirits of the Middle World are a little harder to relate to and work with, often because they seem to have their own agendas. These spirits include the nature spirits, the spirits of the land or the spirits of certain places. For example, your home has a spirit that you can work with to acquire and maintain a harmonious cooperation with. See Exercise #12. Other spirits of the Middle World are the elementals such as the fairies, elves, gnomes, nymphs, and divas, to name just a few. These beings are associated with the four elements: earth, water, air and fire and they embody the energy of the element they represent.

As you gain journeying experience you can learn to work with these spirits in practical ways in gardening, agriculture, landscaping and construction. We can go back to living with nature harmoniously as our ancestors did, treating the animals and the land with respect and veneration. Our ancestors are also Middle World spirits that we can consult with for support and guidance. An even better guide might be a descendent from the future. Since there is no time in non-ordinary reality it is possible to journey forwards and backwards in ordinary time to do problem solving and seek advice. See Exercises #10–#14.

As you journey to the Middle World ask to meet a helping spirit that you can form a lasting, trusting relationship with. When a Middle World spirit volunteers to work with you check your intuitive feelings about that spirit. Does the energy feel vibrant, helpful and positive? If you have any doubts at all, ask your power animal or teacher if that Middle World spirit is the appropriate one for you to work with and follow their recommendation. Remember that one of their jobs is to serve as your guardian in non-ordinary reality. See Exercise #9.

chapter nine
POWER ANIMALS

Once you have connected with your power animal, there are several books that can help you determine the strengths and gifts being brought to you by that animal. While it is tempting to consult the books immediately, first ask your helping spirits how they would like to work with you. Allow your relationship to form without any arbitrary limits imposed by the interpretations of others.

Here are the strengths and characteristics of just a few animals for a quick reference. Remember, your power animal will bring you exactly what you need.

List of Power Animals

Alligator / Crocodile
Alligators and crocodiles are associated with the Great Mother and the feminine essence of birth and life. They represent new beginnings and a time of renewal; an opportunity to begin to unfold and develop some new wisdom. Other characteristics include: protection from manipulation, understanding deceit, maternal protection, and setting boundaries. If alligator or crocodile has come to you look for an opportunity for strong birth and/or initiation that will bring new knowledge and wisdom.

Ant

Ant energy is all about patience, stamina and planning. Ant will bring you support for that major project you've been working on, including self-development. Seek other support from close family, friends and community rather than being isolated. It is time for you to define and design your own destiny instead of trying to please others. Other ant characteristics include: storing for the future, energy and patience needed to complete that project, and communal living. Ant is the promise of success through effort.

Armadillo

If you need protection and help setting your personal boundaries, don't be surprised if armadillo shows up. This implies that you also may need to learn to respect the boundaries of others. Armadillo carries its armor with it, demonstrating that you can carry your protection with you at all times. You define your space and decide what you are willing to experience. Armadillo helps you understand your vulnerabilities. Instead of allowing your empathic abilities the freedom to soak up the feelings and attitudes of others, armadillo will help you discern what is truly yours and what is theirs.

Badger

If badger is your power animal, you can be quick to express your feelings and you do not care what the consequences are. The lesson is that you need to turn your anger and aggression into constructive action without harming others. While badger may seem to be a difficult power animal it is also the protector of rights and spiritual ideas. Badger will certainly help you stop being a victim if you can channel the passion, control and perseverance into creative action. Be grateful for the connection to the earth magic and wisdom and practice being grounded.

Bat

If bat has come to you it is time to face your fears and prepare for change. This is all about the process of transition and how to cope with it, letting go of old habits and attachments that no longer serve you. Other characteristics of bat include: the ability to observe while remaining unseen, invisibility, camouflage, the use of vibrational sound, and the ability to discern the truth in other peoples' words.

Bear

Bear teaches us to go within and search for our own inner wisdom. Solitude, introspection and self-healing are attributes of this power animal. Bear is the creature of visionaries, shamans and mystics. It will help you communicate with the spirits, finding your own answers rather than depending on others. Bear brings us to the place of the inner-knowing where we can find the alternative paths that lead us to our goals. Our ideas are born and nurtured in the death of hibernation and come forth in the spring ready to develop and grow.

Beaver

Beaver is the builder of the animal world, adept at using available resources and working in a cooperative group setting. Beaver will help you be persistent, achieving self-esteem and self-confidence through the completion of tasks. If you tend to procrastinate, Beaver will help you with purposeful and directed activity, reminding you to act on your dreams to make them a reality. When Beaver shows up it is a time for action.

Bee

When Bee shows up it is time to appreciate and enjoy the sweetness of life. Bee's attributes include social skills, organization and cooperation, and prosperity. This is a productive time involving pollination of ideas and bringing plans into fruition. Examine your own productivity for balance and harmony. Being a workaholic can be as detrimental as not being busy enough. Spiritually, Bee wisdom addresses reincarnation and helping earthbound spirits move on to their proper place.

Beetle/Ladybug

The Ladybug is a small beetle that aids in pollination. It carries the Golden Strand that leads to the center of the universe. Ladybug's appearance signals new happiness, often with material gains. Other attributes of Ladybug include: a renewed sense of well-being, granting of wishes, releasing fears and anxieties, and easing away worries. Ladybug aids in spiritual enlightenment and devotional practices.

Blue Jay

Blue Jay teaches us how to use our own power properly and wisely. If you have a situation that has triggered some fear or anxiety, Blue Jay will help you attack it boldly and courageously. It will also help you be vigilant with the ability to discern future trouble areas. Blue Jays have a tremendous ability for survival with the least amount of effort. You can develop your talents and abilities to the fullest or dabble in many fields, knowing a little bit about a lot of things. Be careful of just mimicking others though.

Buffalo/Bison

The bison or buffalo is the symbol of abundance and manifestation. The hump on its back denotes stored resources that can be tapped when needed. When buffalo appears it is a sign that you will have what you need and you should focus on gratitude and appreciation. Buffalo also follows the path of least resistance. Are you making it harder than it needs to be? Allow things to happen and all will be as it should.

Butterfly/Caterpillar

Butterfly represents the energy of transformation and shapeshifting. The butterfly is a powerful symbol of change. It is time to make the changes you've been considering, in yourself, in your life and in your lifestyle. Also be aware of color and joy. Lighten up. Change is a good thing and you can manifest what you want and need. It does not have to be traumatic.

Cougar/Mountain Lion/Puma

If cougar has shown up it is time to learn about power. Test your own and learn to assert it properly. This is about using leadership power wisely and without ego. The key is to balance power, intention and strength, moving forward with faith and courage. This is the time to take control of your life, gaining self-confidence and freedom from guilt. Lead where your heart takes you, without insisting that others follow.

Coyote

Coyote is the great trickster, giving us the ability to laugh at our own mistakes. Working with coyote energy we learn that all things are sacred—yet nothing is sacred. We must find the balance between risk and safety, between wisdom and folly, and between complication and simplicity. Ask yourself what you are really doing and why. Are you fooling others or really just yourself? When things get too serious, the medicine is in laughter. So laugh at yourself and stop the self-sabotage.

Crow

Wherever crows are, there is magic. They are symbols of creation and spiritual strength with the ability to move in space and time. Crow is the keeper of sacred law, guarding all things ethical. When crow appears be very watchful for any omens or signs that will guide you and teach you.

Deer

Deer teaches us the power of gentleness and innocence in thought, word and touch. Combine that with the ability to listen and the power of gratitude and giving for a true understanding of what deer is bringing to you. Trust your instincts and you will develop an ability to detect subtle movements and appearances. Stop trying to force things and use gentleness and love to effect change.

Dolphin/Porpoise

Dolphin is the keeper of the sacred breath of life allowing us to connect with divine energy and wisdom. Dolphin will help you understand the power of rhythm, balance and harmony in your life. Other attributes of dolphin include communication skills, knowledge of the sea and the element of water, and the ability to release intense emotion. It is time to breathe some new life into yourself.

Eagle

Eagle has long been a symbol of spiritual power and illumination. It combines great power, swiftness and strength with balance, dignity and grace. Eagle has keen eyesight, allowing you to see hidden truths, as well as the overall pattern. Eagle will teach you what you need to know to connect with your spirit guides and teachers. Follow your heart and soar to the heights of your greatest dreams.

Elephant

The elephant embodies ancient power, strength and wisdom. It reminds you to not let anything stand in your way of achieving your goals. Determination, patience and confidence are other characteristics of this power animal. Elephants are very family oriented, showing great affection and loyalty to each other. Learning and education are lifelong activities.

Fox

Fox can teach us how to develop the skills of camouflage, invisibility and shapeshifting. Fox has a long history of magic and cunning associated with it. It will help you learn to trust your intuition and be wary of anyone trying to trick or influence you in some way. It's best to blend into the background, move with secrecy and stealth and keep your intentions to yourself.

Frog

Frog will bring you the cleansing you need before your next transformation. This power animal helps you with the ability to be empathic and sensitive to the emotional states of others. It is a symbol of coming into one's own creative power by reminding you of your common bonds with all life.

Hawk

Hawk will teach you to step back and get a greater perspective on a situation by helping you to be observant with keen eyesight and objectivity. Hawk is the messenger about the magic of life that is being brought to you. Pay attention! You are only as powerful as your ability to perceive, receive and use your talents for creativity in the wise use of the opportunities that are coming to you.

Horse/Pony/Mustang

The horse embodies travel, strength and adventure. Other attributes include power, stamina and endurance combined with the freedom to run free and explore your own potential abilities. True power is wisdom found in remembering your journeys. Horse will teach you how to ride in new directions to discover your own freedom and power.

Hummingbird

Hummingbird is all about joy and enjoying the nectar of life. It gives you the flexibility and ability to fly into small places to heal and bring more emotional sweetness into your life. Humming, like the hummingbird, reminds us to find joy in what we do and bring that joy and love to others.

Jaguar

Jaguar helps us reclaim our power, whether it was lost, stolen or broken. The hard work of finding the path amid chaos and learning to move without fear in the darkness will be rewarded. Jaguar also improves psychic ability and the power to see beyond what has been imagined.

Leopard

The leopard is known for its stalking ability, allowing it to approach someone unseen from behind. This attribute is also useful when moving through the shadow worlds. Do not reveal your objective until its completed or this may interfere with its accomplishment. Leopard will help you achieve your goals with strength and vitality.

Lion

Lion teaches us about our role in the family, group, or community. Lion avoids confrontation but is a fierce protector with great strength and courage. When lion has shown up there is an opportunity to awaken to a new sun. You are much stronger than you think you are.

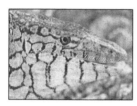

Lizard

Lizard medicine helps you review your dreams before you manifest them physically. The lizard's ability to regenerate that which is lost teaches us to become more detached in life, allowing us to face our fears objectively. Cultivate quiet and stillness until it is time to make your move.

Mole

Mole shows us how to dig out our own treasures in life through our own efforts. It teaches us to trust in what we feel more than in what we see or hear with its understanding of energies and sensitivity to touch and vibration. Mole helps us stay grounded and connected with the energies of the earth.

Moose

Moose is large and majestic, yet graceful. It can move with amazing speed but has an uncanny ability to camouflage itself. It is not shy about sounding off about its feelings and teaches us to share our accomplishments with the world, not in a sense of bragging but in demonstrating our self-esteem. Spiritually, moose finds the soul parts that have been hidden and serves as a bridge to the Elders.

Opossum

Opossum teaches us how to use appearances and the proper utilization of deception. It shows us that the greatest form of protection is to play dead and rely on your instincts to find the best way out of a tight situation. Use strategy instead of confrontation, acting instead of revealing how you really feel. Opossum will help you discover your latent psychic or physical talents.

Otter

Otter helps us connect with feminine energy and woman's healing wisdom. Otter is all about playfulness and curiosity, reminding us that everything is interesting and is worth investigating. Other characteristics include faithfulness, psychic awareness and sensibility without suspicion. This may be the time to stop worrying and simply let things unfold in your life.

Owl

Owl is a symbol for wisdom, freedom and stealth. Owl feathers are silent and it's known as the messenger of secrets and omens to give you answers to any questions you may have. With swift and silent movement and keen eyesight, owl will help you see and hear what others try to hide. With owl as your power animal you have the ability to see behind others' masks and into their souls.

Panther (Black)

The black panther is most powerful in the hours of darkness and in the dead of winter. It has the greatest mysticism associated with it. It is the symbol of darkness, death and rebirth. The black panther helps us know and understand the dark and thus conquer our fear of it, reclaiming our own personal power.

Porcupine

The medicine of porcupine is about faith and trust, innocence and humility. Porcupine embodies the principle of live and let live, of non-interference, of creating your own path and allowing others to follow their own. But when threatened, porcupine is well able to defend itself with barbed quills that stick it to you sharply and intensely. If porcupine is your power animal, move at your own pace rather than responding to pressure from others.

Rabbit/Hare

Rabbit characteristics include fertility, fleetness, and the ability to move with great leaps and hops. It follows periods of quiet and stillness with intense activity, usually generated by fear. As one of the most common prey animals, rabbit must survive using quick-thinking and guile. Use rabbit energy as your guide to facing and moving through your own fears.

Raccoon

Raccoon is extremely adaptable, balancing curiosity with dexterity and disguise. Raccoon loves to explore and will investigate anything without fear. The power of raccoon is in understanding the nature and the magic of masks. The mask is a tool of transformation, allowing us to change what we are to what we want to be. Raccoon can teach you how to mask and disguise and transform yourself.

Skunk

Skunk has very powerful medicine, teaching us how to give respect, expect respect, and demand respect. It's all about self-confidence and reputation. Skunk is fearless, but also very peaceful, helping you understand how to 'walk your talk' and become more assertive. Learn to project, without ego, what you are and respect follows. Stand your ground and don't let yourself be manipulated or pushed around.

Snake/Serpent

Snake energy is about transmuting all poisons, mental, physical, emotional or spiritual. The shedding of the snake's skin is symbolic of the life-death-rebirth cycle and the ability to experience anything willingly and without resistance. Snake signifies a time of movement despite difficult terrain and progress is assured. Be prepared to connect with primitive, elemental and psychic energy.

Spider

Spider is not a cuddly power animal. In fact, it often evokes fear and loathing so most people find it difficult to work with spider. Focus on Spider's qualities that can truly benefit you in your life situations. Spider is the master weaver of the web of fate, providing wisdom, creativity and Divine inspiration. Spider spins its web and waits for the food to come, reminding us that if we do our work, the results will come to us as well.

Squirrel

Squirrels are master puzzle solvers, applying resourcefulness and quick thinking. They are extremely agile and observant, warning others if something different or unusual is happening. Squirrels often seem to be active and busy. Much of their time is spent gathering and storing food for the winter. But they always have time for play, striking a balance between being prepared and using what they have gathered.

Swan

Swan medicine is about self-transformation. Swan teaches us to relax and go with the flow, surrendering to the grace of the rhythm of the universe. Accept your developing intuitive abilities and your power to see into the future. Swan is a powerful bird, but symbolizes grace and stateliness.

Tiger

Tiger will bring you new adventures, awakening passion and energy for life. Tigers are known for their ferocity and power and will bring you strength and will-power in the face of adversity. All of this energy and action may present some challenges, but will certainly introduce some dramatic changes in your life. Use tiger medicine to act in a timely manner without analyzing the situation too much.

Turtle/Tortoise

Turtle is a sign that good news is coming. Its message is power through faith, effort, and tenacity. Turtle is the oldest symbol for Mother Earth and thus helps us to stay grounded. It defends itself through nonviolent means and is all about boundaries, establishing yours and respecting those of others. Turtle helps you be self-reliant and connected to your center and the center of the earth.

Vulture/Buzzard/Condor

Vulture is the symbol of purification. Its medicine restores harmony that has been broken. Vulture soars with grace and ease and serves as a conduit for new vision and perspective.

By using thermal energy, vulture rarely has to flap its wings to soar, teaching us also to use energy efficiently and wisely. Vulture's role as a scavenger fills an extremely valuable and necessary function, serving to keep the environment clean and in balance.

Weasel

Weasel has a wonderful ability to squeeze through narrow spaces and can help you get out of tight spots, maneuvering through and into areas of life that others cannot enter. Weasel is known for its cunning, stealth and keen observation, giving you the ability to see the hidden reasons behind things. Weasel ears hear what is really being said. Other characteristics include great adaptability and ingenuity.

Whale

Whale is an ancient symbol of creation and carries the history of Mother Earth. Although it is the world's largest mammal, it embodies the natural beauty of movement in its element, the oceans of the earth. Whale can teach you how to insulate yourself and use your creative energies more conservatively. The haunting song of the whales helps keep them and you connected to each other and Mother Earth, and teaches you that sounds and frequencies carry balance and healing.

Wolf

Wolf is the pathfinder, the teacher, the forerunner of new ideas. The strength of wolf is in its social and familial values and it has great skill in protecting itself and its extended family. Wolf is extremely intelligent and adaptable, able to outwit enemies by using its keen senses to pass unseen. Wolf medicine is the true spirit of the wilderness; its call is the call of freedom.

Many of these power animal pictures were provided by the www.animalspirits. com web site, which contains many more animal portraits and characteristics.

Dinosaurs

Stegosaurus

The power of stegosaurus is in the use of instinct in being adaptable and non-territorial. It teaches us to let go of the ego and the influence of the mind. It encourages us to be ourselves and let our reputation reflect what we do, not just appearances.

Tyrannosaurus

Tyrannosaurus is well known for its boldness and confrontation skills. Other characteristics include courage, strength, self-esteem and unrelenting pursuit. It teaches us to stand up and face whatever our fears and anxieties are.

Mythical Animals

Dragon

Myths and folklore about dragons abound in legends, tales and prophecies. It is said that the dragon was born of fire and provides a connection to the birth of the universe. A Red Dragon sleeps in the core of the earth, awakening and shifting periodically. The magical properties of dragon include the ability to guard treasure and knowledge, to usher in new cycles of time, to shape and sculpt the earth and to endure to the ending of the world.

Gryphon

The gryphon is one of the oldest magical creatures, depicting the kingly emblems of power and might. Throughout history it has been connected to physical protection and severe revenge tactics. It teaches us of the ability to soar above the fray and make daring leaps of faith. Its magical properties include vigilant protection against evil, a strong grip to guard and protect precious objects, and its untamable nature.

Pegasus

Pegasus, the winged horse, has been associated with protection, boundaries and the ability to fly over any situation. He has also been connected with the Muses, giving inspiration and lightening wisdom to those who create in the arts. To many Pegasus is the embodiment of emotional freedom and the ability to connect with the gods and the spirit world.

Unicorn

Unicorn magic is all about purity, innocence and virginity. It is connected to the forest spirits, fairies, sprites and all of the elementals and nature spirits. Unicorn teaches you to get in touch with your own personal power and use it wisely.

Mythical animal art courtesy of: www.dreslough.com

chapter ten

HOW TO JOURNEY

Preparing to Journey

Shamanic journeys range from simple to complex, from divining the answer to a single question to elaborate healing rituals and ceremonies. Depending on the intention for the journey, the shamanic practitioner may spend hours preparing the space, clearing out any negative or chaotic energy, and welcoming in the helping spirits. Space preparation includes designating a sacred space clean and free of clutter with your drum or rattle close at hand. Clearing involves burning the wild sage plant (dried or formed into a smudge stick), braided sweet grass, or slivers of Palo Santo wood with the intention of driving away any negative energy or uninvited spirits. Welcoming the helping spirits calls in the spirits of the directions: East, South, West, North, Above, Below, and Center; the spirits of the elements: Earth, Water, Air, & Fire; the spirits of Nature; the spirits of all the animals, the plants and Mother Earth. You can also include the spirits of the ancestors and the descendents. Lastly you welcome all of your power animals and teachers even if you will only be working with some of them in this particular journey.

There are no special requirements for preparing to journey. But there are several things the beginner can do to make it easier to relax and enter the shamanic state of consciousness:

1. Designate a space where you can stretch out and make yourself comfortable—but not so comfortable that you fall asleep. You may use a blanket and pillow on the floor or a reclining chair. If you are afraid you will fall asleep simply sit upright in a comfortable chair.

2. Some people burn sage, sweet grass or Palo Santo wood to clear the space of any unwanted energies or spirits. It is similar to burning incense when meditating. You know that you have cleared the space when you set the intention to do so, you focus on the intention as you walk around the space, and when your intuition tells you that the energy feels right.

3. You can use a drum or rattle to help calm your mind

4. Use a bandanna or eye cover to shut out any light that might be distracting

5. Turn off the TV, radio, phone and cell phone—anything that might interrupt the flow of the journey

6. Try to insure that you will not be interrupted by family members or pets

7. Picture in your mind your entry point to either the Lower World or the Upper World and 'see' yourself approaching it

8. State the intention of the journey

9. Start a shamanic drumming tape or CD that contains the recall beat

10. See Exercise #1

Remember that you are entering the shamanic state of consciousness, an altered state similar to deep meditation. So you do NOT listen to a drumming tape or CD when driving your car or performing any task that requires even minimum focus or concentration. Anything that distracts you from concentrating on the intention of the journey will prevent you from achieving the theta brain state that helps you comprehend the information from the spirits.

As you practice journeying, eventually you will be able to drum or rattle for yourself so you can do journeys in nature, or anywhere you won't be disturbed. Shamanic practitioners journey on demand for themselves or for their clients. While it is not necessary to practice journeying every day, though you may if you choose to, it is beneficial to journey on a regular basis. As in every spiritual quest practice gives you familiarity with the process and confidence in the outcome. This is really how you learn to recognize your helping spirits and know that you can trust the information they give you. You become familiar with how each of your helping spirits appears to you, how it interacts with you, and how it conveys information to you.

Journeying to the Lower World

The first step in journeying to the Lower World is deciding how you will get there. There are several possibilities and you may want to try more than one to find what works best for you. If you experience any difficulties, it doesn't necessarily mean that you are doing it wrong. It may just mean that a different route would work better for you. For example, trying to force your way through a close confining tunnel is not a good choice if you are claustrophobic. So choose a portal that you are comfortable with.

It is important in going to the Lower World that you have the sensation of going down into the earth. This can be accomplished by using a familiar cave or animal burrow that opens into a tunnel sloping downward. Or you can dive into a body of water such as a lake, pond or waterfall. Generally, running water like a river or stream is more difficult and the ocean is too large. But if you have a favorite fishing hole in a river that you are comfortable with feel free to try that. Once you have entered the water, look for an opening to the tunnel that slopes downward. If you have a favorite tree or tree stump you can enter the tree through a knothole or imagined doorway and follow the root system downward. Remember that size is relative and that you can imagine yourself fitting easily through any opening. If you have trouble visualizing the tunnel and moving through it you can always fall back on familiar technology. Walk up to an elevator, enter through the door, push the LW button, and exit the elevator into the Lower World. The beginning of your route to the Lower World should be something you can easily visualize and relate to. See Exercise #2.

I was helping a young girl learn how to journey and told her about following the tunnel down to the Lower World. When the drumming stopped with the recall beat I asked about her experience. She said "I was doing fine until the tunnel forked and then I didn't know which one to take." I explained to her that she controls the journey by directing where she enters the tunnel and that she can decide which route to take. "So next time," I said, "just take the right hand fork every time that happens and keep repeating your intention to go to the Lower World." This time she had no trouble because she felt much more in control of the situation.

Another participant in my Introduction to Shamanic Journeying workshop simply could not get to the Lower World no matter which route she tried. She kept getting stuck in the tunnel, even though she could see the light at the end of the tunnel. She just could never get to the mouth of the tunnel and had no sensation of going down to the Lower World. She did have a ready helper though because she already knew who her power animal was. I advised her to call on her power animal to come and meet her in the tunnel and guide her to the Lower World. That made all the difference for her. She felt safe with her power animal and proceeded to have a successful journey.

The important point here is that you don't have to know how to journey to find out who your power animal is. A professional shamanic practitioner may have done a power animal retrieval for you as part of a healing. Your power animal may have come to you in a dream, a meditation, or a vision quest. If you do not know who your power animal is when you first learn to journey, you can wait until you actually get to the Lower World to meet them.

When you have found your route to the Lower World it is time to journey to meet your power animal. See Exercise #3. You can have more than one power animal so don't be surprised if more show up to welcome you. Remember that power animals volunteer to help us as guides and guardians in non-ordinary reality and they may provide a specific strength, such as helping you establish boundaries in personal relationships. You build a relationship with your power animal by asking for their help and by expressing your gratitude to them in return.

A shamanic practitioner told a story at a workshop about teaching children how to journey. After the children had gone to the Lower World and connected with their power animals, one child immediately asked "What do I feed this guy?"

When the recall beat sounds on the drumming CD, ask your power animal to take you back to the tunnel and use the same route to return to ordinary reality. If you have found a successful route to the Lower World, continue to use it every time you journey there. This is part of the discipline of shamanic journeying, ensuring that you always know where you are and that you can trust the information revealed to you. If you are not completely satisfied with the route you are using it is perfectly all right to change it until you are comfortable with the results.

Journeying is not a scary experience because you are always in control of the process. You can exit the journey at any time simply by returning to conscious awareness, provided that you have not used any mind-altering drugs to achieve the journey state. It also helps if you have set an intention or purpose for the journey. That keeps you focused on observing what is happening. You can journey for information and guidance, ask for a healing from your helping spirits, ask your power animals or teachers to show you around non-ordinary reality, or ask your helping spirits to show you how they would like to work with you.

Journeying to the Upper World

While you can journey exclusively to the Lower World to find answers to your questions, it's often a good idea to get another point of view or perspective on the situation. The Upper World is often associated with the mental or spiritual aspects of life. Helping spirits in human form are usually found there, though like power animals, they can go anywhere in non-ordinary reality. These spirits are called teachers and they may be people you recognize, such as religious figures, famous influential people like Gandhi, or other spiritual leaders such as Native American medicine men or wise women. You may even meet fictional characters such as wizards and magicians or mythical beings like dragons and unicorns.

But to meet and work with a teacher you first have to go to the Upper World. Like going to the Lower World, the first step is figuring out the best route for you to take. There are many options available so it's a good idea to try more than one to see which works best for you. Some of the traditional entry routes have included using a tree, a chimney, smoke, and climbing up a mountain side. You can also ask one of your power animals to take you there. Remember, in non-ordinary reality, even earthbound animals can fly.

The route should have a sensation of going up, but the difference from the Lower World is that there is no tunnel to provide the transition into non-ordinary reality. Instead there is a boundary that must be crossed before you are in the Upper World. This boundary or transition point is usually something like a cloud layer or mist that you pass through. If you do not intentionally cross the boundary, you can keep going up into outer space and you are still in this reality. If you have difficulty in visualizing or experiencing a route that takes you through the boundary, you can adapt it to familiar technology and use an escalator or an elevator. Walk up to the elevator, enter through the door, push the UW button, feel the elevator moving up, and exit into the Upper World. When the journey ends you return the same way but push OR for ordinary reality. The beginning of your route to the Upper World should be something you are very familiar with and can easily visualize. See Exercise #5.

If you do not immediately see a landscape, i.e. it is totally empty with either white light or darkness; you may have to proceed to a higher level in the Upper World. This is done by continuing to follow your route upward through another boundary. Keep going until you see, feel or experience some kind of scenery or place. This is different for everyone, so I cannot tell you what you SHOULD see or experience. It is best to not have expectations, but simply relax and accept whatever you encounter. Remember that you control the journey by clearly stating the intention to go to the Upper World. Approach it with a sense of investigation and wonderment and let the magic of shamanic journeying unfold.

When you have found your route to the Upper World it is time to journey to meet your teacher. See Exercise #6. Just as you can have more than one power animal, you can also have more than one teacher. Often a teacher will appear to provide the answer to a particular question and will stay as you work through a situation. Many of us already have a relationship with a familiar religious figure such as Jesus Christ, the Blessed Virgin Mary, a patron saint, or a special angel and it is appropriate to turn to them for support and guidance. But don't be surprised if your teacher is someone you didn't expect, like a deceased relative, an unknown ancestor or a God or Goddess.

A young woman in one of my Introduction to Shamanic Journeying workshops journeyed to the Upper World to find her teacher. When she returned from the journey she asked with a puzzled expression, "Who is Saint Peter?" Several of us commented that she obviously was not raised in the Catholic faith. She had no idea who Saint Peter was or why he would come to her as her teacher. However, the next journey was to go to your teacher and ask for information or advice on a personal question or issue and she received information from him that gave her valuable insights to her problem.

Sometimes, because we view teachers as wise and powerful beings, they may seem more distant and harder to relate to than our power animals. Remember that the intention is to meet a friendly, helpful teacher that you can work with. Always approach all of your helping spirits with respect and gratitude for their assistance.

As you journey to solve problems or get information, your teacher may give you a different answer than you received from your power animal. Many times teachers present the mental or spiritual aspect of the problem or situation, while your power animal addresses the mundane, practical issues. Often, it is valuable to get as many viewpoints as possible to help you make an informed decision. Remember that the information may be presented in many different ways as well. You may receive advice through direct revelation (the spirit talking to you one-on-one), through symbols that have meaning for you, or through images that evoke memories or experiences that you relate to.

Even if you feel a little in awe of your teacher at first, it is still OK to ask for clarification of something you don't understand. Many times the answer to a question leads to many more questions and it is perfectly all right to keep asking for information and examples until you are satisfied. Keep in mind, however, that timing is important. Sometimes, events need to play out before the information and advice you are given makes sense. We cannot control how others act and react so it is best to journey on issues as they affect us. See Exercise #7.

When the recall beat sounds on the drumming CD, come back to ordinary reality by the same route you followed to get to the Upper World. If your power animal took you there, ask them to help you come back. When you have found a route that works well for you continue to use it every time you journey to the Upper World. This discipline will help provide consistency in your shamanic practice.

Journeying to the Middle World

Journeying to the Middle World is different than going to the other realms in non-ordinary reality. This part of non-ordinary reality is most like our physical reality here that we live in every day. The Middle World is like looking at our world through a slightly askew or slanted lens. The landscape is very similar to what we are familiar with and the spirits are known as the 'Little People', the fairies, the elementals and the nature spirits. This realm is also home to many other spirits as well who may not be willing to work with us or who just have their own agendas. This is where ghosts or 'suffering beings' reside, the souls of people who have died that have not moved on to the afterlife. This is also the realm of the spirits of the land who often regard us as visitors, not as 'owners' of the land. *In my classes I give students a lot of journeying experience before introducing them to the Middle World. For the purposes of this book, I recommend that you become comfortable going to the Upper and Lower Worlds before exploring this one.*

But there are advantages to working in the Middle World. This is where the veils between the worlds can be quite thin allowing us to have a greater effect on the situations in our reality. For example, we can help bring harmony and balance back to a polluted waterway or area. We can journey to the spirit of the land where we dwell to ask how to live in peace and harmony with them. See Exercise #12. We can show our appreciation for the land and the nature spirits in the landscaping, gardening and construction work we do. See Exercise #11. And we can learn how to live with the animals and help restore balance to threatened species. By addressing concerns in our environment we also affect the energy in our families and other relationships. There is a shamanic saying "As within, so without; as above, so below". We are always affected by our surroundings and our environment reflects our internal state. As we foster peace, serenity and harmony in our being, that is reflected in our home, and vice versa.

Going to the Middle World is the same technique as going to the Upper and Lower Worlds. You need to have a route that you will follow every time, both going and coming back. And again, you pass through a boundary that defines the veil between ordinary reality and non-ordinary reality. A very good method that several have used successfully is to picture yourself going down three steps into a garden. At the bottom of the third step is a gate that you open to enter the garden. The gate is the boundary that you cross through to enter the Middle World. Returning from the journey at the recall beat, you come back through the gate to this reality. Other routes include following a path over a bridge to the Middle World or entering a thicket or lilac bush and coming out into the Middle World. See Exercise #8.

After you have established your route to the Middle World you need to find a helping spirit who is willing to work with you in this realm. Since Middle World spirits can be unpredictable it is a good idea to take your power animal with you the first time. When you meet a Middle World spirit be prepared for anything: a nature spirit, a tree spirit, a water sprite, a diva, a gnome or an elemental associated with earth, air, fire or water. Ask the spirit to identify itself and ask your power animal if this spirit is a good match for you to work with. If your power animal approves, ask the spirit how they would like you to work with them. What types of power do they have and how can they help you make changes in this world. You will find that many of the Middle World spirits can be enlisted to aid with certain projects, such as cleaning up pollution, planting and growing trees, and restoring the balance to lakes, rivers and streams. See Exercises #10–#12.

How to Set Yourself Up for Successful Journeying

As with any technique or tool the key is USING it! The same is true with the practice of shamanic journeying. The more you journey, the better you get at it. And the more you trust the information and guidance you receive from your spirit helpers. Does that mean that you will get profound insights every time you listen to a drumming CD? Maybe not, but don't underestimate the power of your helping spirits or your ability to tap into your own inner wisdom. This book is about empowering you by giving you the means to make informed decisions so you can chart your own path to happiness and fulfillment. You control your destiny and your mission in this life. This work is about making choices and bringing dreams to fruition. It's about following your heart in a conscious, spiritual way. And it's about your connections to all other things, physically, emotionally and spiritually.

But to accomplish this you need to journey consistently, to maintain contact with the spiritual realms, and keep a journal to record and study how the information is transmitted to you so you can hone your ability to interpret it correctly. Keeping your journal is very exciting and some say intoxicating. There are things that you can do to improve your relationships with your power animals and teachers, and to continue a successful journeying practice. The goal is to use the power of shamanic journeying consistently to give yourself the greatest possibility of successful development in every aspect of your life. Here are a few ways that you can set the stage for valuable, practical journeys that will help you solve problems and regain control of your life.

- **Sacred Space:** It is helpful to set aside a space in your home where you do your journeys. If possible, try to make it as clean and clutter free as you can. You can put pictures or statues of your power animals and teachers around. This is not because they are objects of worship. You are simply honoring your connection and partnership with them and it helps you remember to call on them. You may also store your drum and rattle here along with your drumming CD, blanket and pillow, so everything is close at hand. It should be a space that you enjoy, that is soothing and comforting. A space that you love to go to. I would not recommend journeying in bed—too easy to fall asleep.

- **Timing:** When you journey has a lot to do with your success factor. Waiting until the end of the day when you are physically tired makes it more difficult to stay awake and focused. The objective is to pick a time when you are not in a hurry. You can take the time to relax, calm your mind, and concentrate on the intention of the journey. Make the effort to write down your question in advance so you can determine that it is really what you need/want to get information on. Remember, how you ask the question determines the quality of the information and guidance you receive. There is a fine line between being comfortable and relaxed, and being so comfortable that you tend to fall asleep. You may need to experiment on the best position to use. If you tend to fall asleep, and everyone does occasionally, then sit upright in a chair instead of using a blanket and a pillow. As you become more experienced at journeying, you can take a small rattle with you and go outside. Journeying in nature is fabulous as the connections with our power animals seem much more vibrant and alive. Rattling or drumming for yourself may be distracting at first, but you will soon get used to it.

- **Interruptions:** As much as we love our families and our pets, journeying works much better when they do not interrupt us. There is a flow to the energy of the journey and we need to concentrate and focus on the information we are being given. In fact it's important to write down your impressions immediately when returning from the journey because we forget a lot of it. So, try to minimize possible interruptions. Turn off the phone, send the children outside, put the pets into another room and strive for peace and quiet in your sacred space. However, even your best efforts will not eliminate all interruptions. When something demands your attention in the middle of your journey, remember that you control this process. Simply return your awareness to this reality, pause the drumming CD, take care of the interruption, go back to your sacred space and restart the drumming CD. You can go right back into the journey at the point where you were interrupted, restate the intention of the journey and resume as if nothing happened.

- **Frequency:** It is not necessary to journey every day, unless you feel the need for additional guidance. Once or twice a week is a good way to establish your routine. Most important is that you LOOK for reasons to journey. What is happening in your life that you could use some help with? What problems and issues are you struggling with that you wish you could change? As you find that the shamanic journeying method really does get results, you will be more inclined to use it on a regular basis. Journeying is a very individual process. You will determine what is right for you. A good journey to do occasionally is going to your power animals, teachers and Middle World spirits just to say hi and let them know how grateful you are for their help and support, instead of just going when you need something. Remember, you can also ask them to come and be with you in this reality too.

- **Remembering your journey:** As mentioned earlier, we tend to forget a lot of what happens in our journeys because there's so much going on. So it is important to train ourselves to pay attention to details and remember that all of our senses give us clues to the answer we are seeking. That is also why it pays to write down your impressions immediately after returning to this reality. Another way to train yourself to focus and concentrate is to narrate your journey as you are doing it. This is a great way to discover just how much detail you are missing as it happens. To set this up you need headphones for the drumming CD and a recorder of some kind. I use a small digital recorder with a microphone that clips onto my lapel. Then I talk into the recorder as things are happening in the journey. This may be distracting at first, but it is one of the best ways I know to make sure you are getting all of the information the spirits are giving you. As you listen to the recording, you will be amazed at what you have already forgotten. Many times too, the journey doesn't really end at the recall beat. Even though you return to this reality, you may still be getting insights and information days later. These 'Ah Ha' moments are where you start to make connections that you didn't see before.

- **Tracking your progress:** This book has many exercises that will help you keep track of where you are in learning this process. I encourage you to use what you need and move at your own pace. If you have problems and issues that are causing turmoil in your life right now, you can choose to journey just to the Lower World and work with your power animals to get you started on regaining control. Then you can add journeys to the Upper World to get another perspective from your teachers. You can use the examples included here that best fit your circumstances to gain journeying experience and trust in your helping spirits. As you become familiar with the power of the shamanic journey and the wealth of advice and guidance that is available, you may want to investigate attending classes or workshops on integrating shamanic practice into your lifestyle. There are many excellent shamanic teachers and practitioners throughout the world. Many are listed on the websites www. shamanicteachers.com, www.shamanicstudies.org, www.shamansociety.org, and www.shamanportal.org.

chapter eleven

QUESTIONS ABOUT SHAMANIC JOURNEYING & EMPOWERMENT

What is Shamanism and what can it do for me?

Shamanism is an ancient traditional system used for healing and solving problems for individuals and communities. Traditional indigenous shamans were the spiritual leaders of their tribe, serving as healers, historians, storytellers and interfaces with the spirit world. In our culture, shamanism co-exists very well with our urban lifestyle, complex technology and mainstream religion. Modern men and women have quickly learned and adopted the basic techniques for seeing and journeying into the spirit world, by going into an altered state of consciousness, to obtain information and advice to solve personal problems. You can do this as well by following the methods in this book. You can use the power of the shamanic journey to connect with spirit helpers in the form of animals and teachers, and receive guidance and advice on how to solve your personal problems and issues.

What are helping spirits and how do I identify them?

In shamanism, helping spirits are known as power animals and teachers. They reside in the spirit realm or non-ordinary reality. Humans interact with the spirits, who serve as our guides and sources of knowledge, by going to non-ordinary reality in a shamanic journey. We make a connection with them by journeying with the intention of finding our power animal or teacher. At first we know that a power animal or teacher is a helping spirit by asking them in the journey, "Are you my power animal?" Or, "Are you my teacher?" The spirit will indicate in some way that, yes, they have come to help us in our quest for information, advice or healing. As we continue to work with them in subsequent journeys, our power animals and teachers become our trusted guides and partners. See Exercises #3 and #6.

How do I get information in a journey from a helping spirit?

The shamanic journey is a way of accessing knowledge and information beyond what we can get with our senses here in our physical world. Our helping spirits, power animals and teachers, give us information in many ways. One way is telepathically, where you receive the thought in your mind. You may also 'hear' or 'see' the information in your mind. The important thing to remember is that everyone receives the information in their own way. Journeying is a very individual process. There is no right or wrong way. There is only your way, which is different from my way. Usually the spirits do not give us a black/white, yes or no answer to our question. They give us metaphors, examples and symbols that only we can interpret, through the means of direct revelation. All of the symbols and examples mean something to us, they remind us of something or they illustrate something we already know. It is up to us to figure out the whole picture. See Exercises #4 and #7.

What is Direct Revelation and how do I know I'm experiencing it?

The power of the shamanic journey is that we receive information directly from our helping spirit in the form of metaphors, examples and symbols that only we can interpret. The information is not re-layed to us by a medium or psychic, nor do we have to have help figuring out what it means. Direct revelation is a one-on-one infor-mation exchange between us and our helping spirits. We journey to non-ordinary reality with the intention of asking our helping spirits for guidance or advice to solve a personal problem. You know you are experiencing it when you receive information in a journey that gives you insight or a practical method to solve a problem that you are struggling with. As you gain journeying experience, you will see how this powerful technique empowers you to make your own deci-sions and chart your own path to fulfillment and happiness. If you have impeccable technique and you have established a good working relationship with your power animal or teacher, then you can trust the information you receive.

How are totem animals different from power animals?

A totem is any natural object, being or animal with which we feel closely associated and whose attributes and energy are related to our life in some way. You may have had a special affinity for a particular type of animal all your life. The dog, the cat, the horse or another animal may have fascinated you since childhood. So you might ex-pect this special animal to be your power animal or helping animal spirit. However, for shamanic practice this may not be the case, at least not in the way you expect. Power here means spiritual power that comes from inherent knowledge, information or wisdom that the power animal willingly shares with you. Your power animal vol-unteers to come and help you and brings you the strengths and char-acteristics you need to bolster your own personal power. Through-out your lifetime you can have many power animals. They are with you for a while to fill a special need or purpose. An example is to solve a particular problem, like a remodeling project that has had nu-merous setbacks, mistakes and missed deadlines. Doing a journey on this issue to find out what can be done to change the circumstances may result in Beaver, the master builder, volunteering to help oversee the spiritual energy around the project. Journeying to Beaver in this situation will provide the insights needed to improve the energetic flow of the project. As you continue to work with Beaver and things on the remodeling site improve, you will know that you can trust the information you receive.

How do I know that I'm not just making this all up?

Our culture has taught us throughout our lives that there is no spirit world, that only what you can see, feel, hear, taste and smell is real. Anything else exists solely in our imagination. Most of us, however, do believe that current scientific experiments can measure phenomena that we cannot experience with our five senses; things that were considered impossible just a few years ago. In fact, scientific experimentation is beginning to 'discover' things that a lot of us knew instinctively all along. The best way to evaluate the validity of the information and guidance you receive in your shamanic journeys is on the basis of your results. Was the information helpful? Did you receive insights and make connections that were hidden from you before? Shamanism is a results-oriented system. As you continue your journeying practice, you will experience useful and beneficial results. You direct the journey by defining the intention or guidance that you are seeking, but your helping spirits determine the information you receive and how you receive it.

What's the 'best' way to journey?
How do I know I'm doing it right?

There really is no 'best' way to journey. In fact, there is no right way and no wrong way. Everyone does it differently, so it is just how you do it as opposed to how I do it. Some people see very clear pictures, almost like videos, when they get information. Others 'hear' the information in their mind and others just feel or know what is going on and what the answer is. All of these are perfectly valid ways of getting the answer to your question. I cannot tell you how to feel or what to feel. Your journeying experience is unique to you. There are, however, some things you can do to prepare to journey when you are getting started. You want to achieve a relaxed state, but not so relaxed that you fall asleep. See Exercise #1. Follow the exercises in this book to get started and track your progress as you gain experience. You know you are doing it right when you get information, answers and guidance that make a positive change in your life.

Is there anything I need to be careful of when I journey?

Any self-empowerment method or technique can have both positive and negative effects. Your shamanic journey is directed by you by clearly stating the intention or reason for the journey. In other words, intention is everything. When first starting to journey, I recommend going to the Lower World and finding your power animal. It is reassuring to know that your power animal's job is to serve as your guide and guardian in non-ordinary reality. It is a good practice to invite your power animal along even when you go to the Upper World to find your teacher and when you explore the Middle World. Whenever you have a question about how something feels or how it should be, you can always ask your power animal to check it out. The best way to ensure that you will get optimal positive results is to have a clear intention for the journey with a well-defined question that you want information on.

How do I know where I'm at in non-ordinary reality? The Lower World? The Upper World? The Middle World?

In shamanism, non-ordinary reality or the spirit realm has three different worlds: the Lower World, the Upper World and the Middle World. Each has its own energy and 'feels' different. I cannot tell you how it feels, because everyone experiences it differently. In going to the Lower World You have a sense of going down. In going to the Upper World you have a sense of going up. In going to the Middle World you proceed horizontally on a path that stays fairly level. In each case, however, there is a boundary or a transition point that you must cross or go through to reach non-ordinary reality. You define what this boundary looks like for you, so you know it each time you journey. It always stays the same for you. Each person has their own concept of what this boundary looks and feels like. See Exercises #2, #5 and #8.

How do I establish a relationship with my helping spirits?

Like any good friends, your helping spirits expect and appreciate your consideration and respect. Don't just go to them when you want something. Journey to them sometimes with the intention of just saying hi and expressing your gratitude for their help and support. Invite them to come to you in this world and experience your activities. Some people take their power animals with them anytime they drive somewhere. I call on all of my helping spirits every time I teach a class or give a lecture. You can put pictures or statues of your power animals and teachers in your sacred space where you journey. And you can wear a charm or pendant in its honor. The point is that you are aware of your helping spirits all of the time, not just when you journey. The more you do this, the more you can trust the information you get from them. Eventually, you will even get information, signs and omens from them in this world without having to journey.

Where do I go from here? How do I start and maintain a shamanic spiritual practice?

The best thing is to keep solving your problems and issues by using the shamanic journey to get information, guidance and support. As you experience the positive results achieved through using the shamanic system, you will naturally think of journeying more often. You will begin to experience more control in your life, more empowered to define and direct your life mission. Instead of constantly reacting to influences beyond your control and feeling powerless to effect change, you will be able to take a more proactive approach and be able to make informed decisions for the benefit of all concerned. Life becomes more vibrant ... and fun ... and worth living again. Eventually, you may want to expand your exploration of the world of shamanism. Your relationships with your helping spirits goes to a deeper level and you feel a connection with all things. There are several books available and many shamanic teachers that provide in-depth courses in shamanic practice. See Resources.

chapter twelve

MY SHAMANIC JOURNEY

Seven Gifts from Keeping Your Shamanic Journal

1. You learn the "Language of Your Personal Universe"

2. You develop relationships with your Power Animals, Guides and Teachers whom you can call upon for the rest of your life

3. You realize you are in control of your reality

4. You feel empowered in the physical realm regardless of external circumstances

5. You have an exciting "secret place" in your life that offers you somewhere to go anytime and anyplace

6. You connect with the deeper part of yourself that you know you can implicitly trust always

7. You remember the "ancient echoes" that have called out to your entire life and you realize you have finally found your true Spiritual Home

Exercise 1: Preparing To Journey

The purpose of this exercise is to prepare the setting and yourself before actually doing a shamanic journey.

Before attempting your first shamanic journey it is helpful to 'set the stage' and prepare yourself to enter the theta brain state. There are frequencies/rhythms which when dominant in the brain correlate with a specific state of mind. There are generally 4 groupings of brain waves:

1. Beta waves range between 13–40 HZ. The beta state is associated with peak concentration, heightened alertness and visual acuity.

2. Alpha waves range between 7–12 HZ. This is a place of deep relaxation, but not quite meditation. In Alpha, we begin to access the wealth of creativity that lies just below our conscious awareness—it is the gateway, the entry point that leads into deeper states of consciousness.

3. Theta waves range between 4–7 HZ. It is known as the twilight state which we normally only experience fleetingly as we rise up out of the depths of delta upon waking, or drifting off to sleep. In theta we are in a waking dream, vivid imagery flashes before the mind's eye and we are receptive to information beyond our normal conscious awareness. During the Theta state many find they are capable of comprehending advanced concepts and relationships that become incomprehensible when returning to Alpha or Beta states. Theta has also been identified as the gateway to learning and memory. Theta meditation increases creativity, enhances learning, reduces stress and awakens intuition and other extrasensory perception skills.

4. Delta waves range between 0–4 HZ. Delta is associated with deep sleep.

Referenced from http://www.web-us.com/primitivebeats.htm, Intelegen, Inc. 1995–2008.

So how do you achieve the Theta state of mind? Modern shamanic practitioners usually achieve the theta state through drumming or rattling. Experienced meditators can train themselves to achieve this state through meditation, and currently there are many brain entrainment audio programs available to help you experience

Theta. However, your best practice will be to achieve Theta through drumming or rattling—it will program your mind to reach this state whenever you hear the drumming or rattling, and you will be honoring the Shamanic tradition of journeying as you do so.

While there are no actual requirements for preparing to journey, you may find the following suggestions helpful.

1. Select a spot where you can lie down or use a reclining chair. Don't journey when you are tired, but if you think you may fall asleep just sit upright in a comfortable chair.

2. Pick a time when you will not be interrupted by family members. Put pets in another room.

3. Turn off the TV, radio and phone.

4. You can choose to burn sage, sweet grass or Palo Santo wood, but it is not necessary. You can burn incense, but that is associated more with meditation than with shamanic journeying. If you meditate, you may get confused on what you are doing.

5. Make sure that you have a shamanic drumming CD ready to turn on remotely. One is included with this book and there are many others available on the internet or at specialty stores nationwide.

6. Close your eyes and think of the intention for the journey. What is it you want to accomplish in this journey? You can use an eye covering to shut out any distracting light.

7. If you have a question you want answered, define how you will ask the question in an open way to get the most information, i.e. What do I need to know about_____?

8. Think of your portal for entering either the Lower World, the Middle World or the Upper World. Picture it clearly in your mind, recalling all the details you can.

9. Picture yourself approaching the portal. See it clearly in your mind.

10. When you are ready, start the drumming CD and enter the portal.

11. Allow yourself to just flow—go with your imagination—do not censor. Just become like a curious child filled with wonder and know that the more you feel like you are "making it up," the more authentic it probably is. After several experiences, you will become more comfortable with the process and the information ... it is like visiting a new land and after awhile you become more familiar with the energy and landmarks.

Possible issues

1. How do I know the space is right? Any place where you feel comfortable is right for you.

2. How do I know the energy is clear? It's your place. You know how it normally feels. Your intuition will tell you if you need to burn sage or something else. Trust what your inner sense is telling you.

3. I can't clear my mind: Remember that journeying is not the same as meditation. It is normal to have distracting thoughts. The way to stay focused is to repeat the intention of the journey and/or the question that you want answered both before and during the journey.

4. I think the drumming is distracting: If you are used to meditating you may find the drumming distracting at first. Keep practicing and eventually the drumming fades into the background and is no longer an issue.

Record your impressions immediately along with any adjustments you want to make before you forget your experiences. The more you journey, the more information you will receive and recording everything—impressions, thoughts, images, memories—will help you begin to understand the Language of Your Own Personal Universe. Let me emphasize that "Journeying & Journaling," go hand in hand—and will enrich your experience and validate the information you receive from the realms of non-ordinary reality.

Exercise 2: Finding Your Route to the Lower World

As with all your journeys, the more you just flow and trust, the richer your journey will be. It is good to become like a child and just allow yourself to flow—without censoring.

The purpose of this exercise is to explore your chosen route to the Lower World by traveling there and back again.

Your route to the Lower World involves a portal or opening, a tunnel or means of going down into the earth and an end of the tunnel which opens onto some kind of landscape. The portal should be something you are very familiar with and can easily visualize. As you enter the portal in your mind, use your imagination to create an opening to a tunnel sloping downward. Visualize the tunnel as being wide, roomy, lighted and inviting so you can easily walk through it. As you descend through the tunnel, speed does not matter. Remember that you control this process so visualize the end or opening of the tunnel ahead of you. Mentally 'talk' yourself through the tunnel by saying "Now I am at the end of the tunnel looking out into the Lower World. Now I am stepping out of the tunnel and looking at the landscape here." After checking out the scenery, turn around and return to ordinary reality by coming back the same way. The landscape can be anything, even complete darkness so don't be dismayed by what you encounter. Simply make a note of it and return. Going through the portal, feeling yourself traveling down, coming out into some kind of landscape and returning is a successful journey!

Preparing to journey to the Lower World

1. Select a spot where you can lie down or use a reclining chair. Don't journey when you are tired, but if you think you may fall asleep just sit upright in a comfortable chair.

2. Pick a time when you will not be interrupted by family members. Put pets in another room.

3. Turn off the TV, radio and phone.

4. You can choose to burn sage, sweet grass or Palo Santo wood, but it is not necessary. You can burn incense, but that is associ-

ated more with meditation than with shamanic journeying. If you meditate, you may get confused on what you are doing.

5. Make sure that you have a shamanic drumming CD ready to turn on remotely. One is included with this book and there are many others available on the internet or at specialty stores nationwide.

6. Close your eyes and think of the intention for the journey. You are finding your route to go to the Lower World. You can use an eye covering to shut out any distracting light.

7. Think of your portal for entering the Lower World. Picture it clearly in your mind, recalling all the details you can.

8. Picture yourself approaching the portal. See it clearly in your mind.

9. When you are ready, start the drumming CD and enter the portal.

Possible issues

1. **Choosing a difficult portal:** If you find that you are having difficulty with your choice of portal, you can change your entry point as often as you want. When you find one that you are comfortable with, that one should be used consistently.

2. **Getting stuck in the tunnel:** It's your tunnel. You control what it looks like, how it feels and how long it is. 'Talk' yourself through it. You can also use a different route such as a slide, a waterfall or an elevator.

3. **Everything is dark:** The spirits may be asking you to use all of your senses instead of relying just on sight. Everything you see, touch, smell, hear or just 'know' gives you information. What are your other senses telling you?

4. **You met an animal:** This may be your power animal. You'll find out in the next journey.

Journey & Journal

Record your impressions immediately before you forget your experiences. Are you keeping updates in your journal? Remember, the information you receive when journeying is often like information you get in a dream—as you return to the beta state of mind much of the information fades and is often ultimately lost. Therefore, be sure to make it a habit to journey and journal immediately afterward.

_____

_____

_____

_____

_____

_____

_____

_____

_____

_____

_____

_____

_____

_____

_____

_____

_____

_____

_____

_____

_____

_____

_____

Exercise 3: Meeting Your Power Animal

One of the most exciting experiences you will have is when you identify and develop a relationship with your power animal or animals. They are your guides to the Lower World who will help you understand and resolve life issues.

The purpose of this exercise is to go to the Lower World and meet a power animal.

Begin the journey by approaching your portal in your mind. State the intention of the journey "The intention for this journey is to go to the Lower World and meet my power animal." Start the drumming CD (20 min track). Go through the portal and enter the tunnel. State the intention of the journey a second time "The intention for this journey is to go to the Lower World and meet my power animal." Mentally 'talk' yourself through the tunnel and step out into the Lower World. State the intention for the journey for the third time. This keeps you focused on your reason for being there. Because you have been so clear about your intention, an animal will appear before you. Ask "Are you my power animal?" If the animal indicates in some way that it is, then ask it to show you around. If it says or indicates "No, I'm not," then ask it to take you to your power animal. Keep asking for a clear indication from your power animal and keep looking for non-verbal signs and body language. When the recall beat sounds, ask your power animal to take you back to the tunnel opening, thank them, and return up the tunnel.

Preparing to journey to find your power animal

1. Select a spot where you can lie down or use a reclining chair. Don't journey when you are tired, but if you think you may fall asleep just sit upright in a comfortable chair.

2. Pick a time when you will not be interrupted by family members. Put pets in another room.

3. Turn off the TV, radio and phone.

4. You can choose to burn sage, sweet grass or Palo Santo wood, but it is not necessary. You can burn incense, but that is associ-

ated more with meditation than with shamanic journeying. If you meditate, you may get confused on what you are doing.

5. Make sure that you have a shamanic drumming CD ready to turn on remotely. One is included with this book and there are many others available on the internet or at specialty stores nationwide.

6. Close your eyes and think of the intention for the journey. You are journeying to the Lower World to find your power animal. You can use an eye covering to shut out any distracting light.

7. Think of your portal for entering the Lower World. Picture it clearly in your mind, recalling all the details you can.

8. Picture yourself approaching the portal. See it clearly in your mind.

9. When you are ready, start the drumming CD and enter the portal.

Possible issues

1. **You see lots of animals:** Focus on the animal that seems to stay with you or that stands out in some way, especially if it indicates it is trying to communicate with you. This is where you are learning to trust your intuition—you may feel an energy field or vibration from this particular animal—or an auric field—trust that the power animal that is for you on this journey will appear and make itself known.

2. **You only see part of the animal:** Sometimes you will only see a hoof or a horn or an eye. Remember that you must use all of your senses. What do you 'feel' about this animal?

3. **More than one animal responds:** If more than one animal volunteers to help you, that is a good thing. Thank them for coming and ask them to show you around. Like angels, sometimes you will have a "team" of animals appear to help you -- if that is the case, bless them, thank them, and then mentally ask each of them how they can best help -- sometimes differ-

ent animals will help in different ways for complex issues --
much like a committee meeting -- this is your Animal Council.

4. **It takes a long time:** If you are not seeing any animals or they
   don't seem to be responding keep repeating the intention of
   the journey. And relax!

Journey & Journal

Record your impressions immediately before you forget your experiences. Are you keeping updates in your journal? Remember, the
information you receive when journeying is often like information
you get in a dream—as you return to the beta state of mind much of
the information fades and is often ultimately lost. Therefore, be sure
to make it a habit to journey and journal immediately afterward.

_____

_____

_____

_____

_____

_____

_____

_____

_____

_____

_____

_____

_____

_____

_____

_____

_____

_____

Exercise 4: Asking Your Power Animal a Question

Before you start to journey set your intention for the journey and define the question you wish to ask. Your intention is to journey to the Lower World and ask your power animal a question. The question can be anything you want information on. Questions should be open ended, rather than yes or no questions. *The traditional rule is one question—one journey.* If you ask questions on more than one topic it's difficult to sort out which information goes with which question. The question should also be simple and specific, no 'and/or' phrases.

Example question formats

- What can you tell me about …
- What is my next step regarding …
- How can you help me with …
- What do I need to know about … (This can be one of the most powerful information gathering questions—and I recommend you use this as a core question in all of your journeys).

After you have defined your question you can prepare to journey.

1. Find a comfortable position so you can relax
2. It helps to have an eye shade to shut out the light
3. Picture your entry point to the Lower World clearly in your mind
4. Start the drumming tape or some other percussion tape (rattle, Tibetan bowls, chanting, etc.) (10 min or 20 min track)
5. State your intention and question in your mind
6. Picture yourself approaching your tunnel entrance
7. Enter your tunnel
8. State your intention and question again while in the tunnel

9. Look ahead to the light at the end of the tunnel; come out of the tunnel into a landscape
10. Look around for your (a) power animal and again state your intention and question to your power animal
11. Go with your power animal as information is presented and your question is answered
12. When the recall beat sounds thank your PA and ask him/her to take you back to the mouth of your tunnel
13. Come back up the tunnel during the double time beat
14. Return to ordinary reality
15. Record the details of your journey immediately so you don't forget them

Interpreting your journey

What did your power animal do when you asked the question? Did you receive information telepathically in your mind or did you 'see' something? What was the 'feel' or energy of the information you received? Did your power animal take you somewhere and what was the scenario you experienced there? What did you experience through all of your senses?

This is an exciting part of your journeying to these non-ordinary realms. You are learning how your inner self communicates with these guides, and as you journey and journal you will come to learn and be able to interpret how your Inner Self is communicating. No two people will journey in the same way—and no two people will usually receive information in the same way—just as your intuition communicates with you in unique symbols, thoughts, feelings, and visuals.

Journey & Journal

Record your impressions immediately before you forget your experiences. Are you keeping updates in your journal? Remember, the information you receive when journeying is often like information you get in a dream—as you return to the beta state of mind much of the information fades and is often ultimately lost. Therefore, be sure to make it a habit to journey and journal immediately afterward.

_____

_____

_____

_____

_____

_____

_____

_____

_____

_____

_____

_____

_____

_____

_____

_____

_____

_____

_____

_____

_____

_____

_____

_____

_____

_____

Exercise 5: Finding Your Route to the Upper World

The purpose of this exercise is to explore your chosen route to the Upper World by traveling there and back again.

Your route to the Upper World involves a path or a route that travels up or gives you the feeling of going up. This can be a trail climbing up a mountainside or smoke going up a chimney. You can ride up a rainbow or a tornado. You can ask your power animal to fly you there. But there must be a boundary of some sort that you pass through to enter the Upper World. This boundary usually takes the form of a cloud layer or mist that you enter and pass through. As you ascend on your route, speed does not matter. Remember that you control this process so visualize the boundary ahead of you. Mentally 'talk' yourself along the route by saying "Now I am at the point where my path enters the cloud layer. I am going through the cloud/mist layer and stepping out into the Upper World. Now I am standing above the cloud layer and looking at the landscape here." After checking out the scenery, turn around and return to ordinary reality by coming back the same way. The landscape can be anything, even complete darkness, so don't be dismayed by what you encounter. Simply make a note of it and return. Starting on your path, feeling yourself traveling up, coming through the boundary into some kind of landscape and returning is a successful journey!

Preparing to journey to the Upper World

1. Find a comfortable position so you can relax
2. It helps to have an eye shade to shut out the light
3. Picture your entry point to the Upper World clearly in your mind
4. Start the drumming tape or some other percussion tape (rattle, Tibetan bowls, chanting, etc.) (10 min or 20 min track)
5. State your intention to go to the Upper World and return in your mind
6. Picture yourself approaching your route to the Upper World

7. Look ahead to the boundary and mentally 'talk' yourself through the boundary

8. Look around at the landscape

9. When the recall beat sounds come back by the same route during the double time beat

10. Return to ordinary reality

11. Record the details of your journey immediately so you don't forget them

Possible issues

1. **Choosing a difficult path:** You can change your entry route as often as you want. When you find one that you are comfortable with, that one should be used consistently.

2. **Can't find the boundary:** This is your route. You control what it looks like, how it feels and how long it takes. 'Talk' yourself through it. You can also use a different route such as an airplane, a hot-air balloon, an escalator or an elevator.

3. **Everything is white or dark:** The spirits may be asking you to use all of your senses instead of relying just on sight. Everything you see, touch, smell, hear or just 'know' gives you information. What are your other senses telling you?

4. **You met a person or spiritual figure:** This may be your teacher. You'll find out in the next journey.

Journey & Journal

Record your impressions immediately before you forget your experiences. Are you keeping updates in your journal? Remember, the information you receive when journeying is often like information you get in a dream—as you return to the beta state of mind much of the information fades and is often ultimately lost. Therefore, be sure to make it a habit to journey and journal immediately afterward.

Exercise 6: Meeting Your Teacher

The purpose of this exercise is to go to the Upper World and meet a teacher.

Begin the journey by approaching your upward route in your mind. State the intention of the journey "The intention for this journey is to go to the Upper World and meet my teacher." Start the drumming CD (20 min track). Follow your route upward and state the intention of the journey a second time "The intention for this journey is to go to the Upper World and meet my teacher." Mentally 'talk' yourself through the boundary (cloud layer) and step out into the Upper World. State the intention for the journey for the third time. This keeps you focused on your reason for being there. Because you have been so clear about your intention, a teacher will appear to meet you. Ask "Are you my teacher?" If the figure indicates in some way that it is, then ask how you are to work with them. If it says "No, I'm not," then ask them to take you to your teacher. Keep asking for a clear indication from your teacher and keep looking for non-verbal signs and body language. Your teacher may be someone you recognize. Ask what they would like you to call them. At the recall beat, ask your teacher to take you back to the starting point, thank them, and return by the same route.

Preparing to journey to find your teacher

1. Find a comfortable position so you can relax
2. It helps to have an eye shade to shut out the light
3. Picture your entry point to the Upper World clearly in your mind
4. Start the drumming tape or some other percussion tape (rattle, Tibetan bowls, chanting, etc.) (20 min track)
5. State your intention to find your teacher in your mind
6. Picture yourself approaching your route to the Upper World
7. State your intention again while on your route to the Upper World

8. Look ahead to the boundary; Pass through the boundary into a landscape

9. Look around for your teacher

10. When the recall beat sounds thank your teacher and ask him/her to take you back to your route home

11. Come back via the same route during the double time beat

12. Return to ordinary reality

13. Record the details of your journey immediately so you don't forget them

Possible issues

1. **You see lots of people:** Focus on the person that seems to stay with you or that stands out in some way, especially if he/she indicates they are trying to communicate with you. If no one seems to notice you, stay on your path going up further to the next level, by passing through another boundary or cloud layer.

2. **You don't see anyone:** Sometimes you have to go to a higher level to meet someone. Remember that you must use all of your senses. Do you 'feel' as if there is anyone there?

3. **More than one teacher responds:** If more than one teacher volunteers to help you, that is a good thing. Thank them for coming and ask them how they want to work with you.

4. **It takes a long time:** If you are not seeing any teachers or they don't seem to be responding keep repeating the intention of the journey. And relax!

Journey & Journal

Record your impressions immediately before you forget your experiences. Are you keeping updates in your journal? Remember, the information you receive when journeying is often like information you get in a dream—as you return to the beta state of mind much of the information fades and is often ultimately lost. Therefore, be sure to make it a habit to journey and journal immediately afterward.

_____

_____

_____

_____

_____

_____

_____

_____

_____

_____

_____

_____

_____

_____

_____

_____

_____

_____

_____

_____

_____

_____

_____

_____

_____

_____

_____

Exercise 7: Asking Your Teacher a Question

Before you start to journey set your intention for the journey and define the question you wish to ask. Your intention is to journey to the Upper World and ask your teacher a question. The question can be anything you want information on. Questions should be open ended, rather than yes or no questions. *The traditional rule is one question—one journey.* If you ask questions on more than one topic it's difficult to sort out which information goes with which question. The question should also be simple and specific, no 'and/or' phrases.

Example question formats

- What can you tell me about ...
- What is my next step regarding ...
- How can you help me with ...
- What do I need to know about ... (This can be one of the most powerful information gathering questions—and I recommend you use this as a core question in all of your journeys).

After you have defined your question you can prepare to journey

1. Find a comfortable position so you can relax
2. It helps to have an eye shade to shut out the light
3. Picture your route to the Upper World clearly in your mind
4. Start the drumming tape or some other percussion tape (rattle, Tibetan bowls, chanting, etc.) (10 min or 20 min track)
5. State your intention and question in your mind
6. Picture yourself on your path or route to the Upper World
7. Picture the boundary ahead as a cloud or mist layer
8. State your intention and question again while approaching the boundary
9. Go into and through the boundary; come out of the cloud layer or boundary into a landscape

10. Look around for your teacher and again state your intention and question to your teacher

11. Go with your teacher as information is presented and your question is answered

12. When the recall beat sounds, thank your teacher and ask him/her to take you back to the boundary

13. Come back down via the same route you used to go up during the double time beat

14. Return to ordinary reality

15. Record the details of your journey immediately so you don't forget them

Interpreting your journey

What did your teacher do when you asked the question? Did you receive information telepathically in your mind or did you 'see' something? What was the 'feel' or energy of the information you received? Did your teacher take you somewhere and what was the scenario you experienced there? What did you experience through all of your senses?

Journey & Journal

Record your impressions immediately before you forget your experiences. Are you keeping updates in your journal? Remember, the information you receive when journeying is often like information you get in a dream—as you return to the beta state of mind much of the information fades and is often ultimately lost. Therefore, be sure to make it a habit to journey and journal immediately afterward.

_____

_____

_____

_____

_____

Exercise 8: Finding Your Route to the Middle World

It is best to practice journeying by becoming familiar with the Lower World and establishing a good working relationship with your power animal(s) first. When you are comfortable in this realm you can start going to the Upper World to work with your teacher(s). After you have experienced the different energies of these worlds you can go to the Middle World to find your helping spirit(s) there.

Lower World → Upper World → Middle World
The purpose of this exercise is to explore your chosen route to the Middle World by traveling there and back again.

Your route to the Middle World involves a path or a way that travels horizontally through an entry point or portal. To cross the veil to non-ordinary reality there must be a boundary of some sort that you pass through to enter the Middle World. A successful method used by many is to go down three steps into a garden. At the bottom of the third step is a gate that you go through. This gate is the boundary or portal to the Middle World. Remember that you control this process so visualize the boundary ahead of you. 'Talk' yourself along the route by saying "Now I am going down the three steps. I am going through the gate at the bottom of the steps and stepping out into the garden in the Middle World." After checking out the scenery, turn around and return to ordinary reality by coming back the same way, through the gate and back up the three steps. The landscape may start as a garden but then can change to anything, so don't be dismayed by what you encounter. Simply make a note of it and return. There are other types of paths you can try as well, such as one that crosses over a river or a path that goes through a thicket of bushes. Starting on your path, feeling yourself going through the boundary into some kind of landscape and returning is a successful journey!

Preparing to journey to the Middle World
1. Find a comfortable position so you can relax
2. It helps to have an eye shade to shut out the light

3. Picture your entry point to the Middle World clearly in your mind

4. Start the drumming tape or some other percussion tape (rattle, Tibetan bowls, chanting, etc.) (10 min or 20 min track)

5. State your intention to go to the Middle World and return in your mind

6. Picture yourself approaching your route to the Middle World

7. Look ahead to the boundary and 'talk' yourself through the boundary

8. Look around at the landscape

9. When the recall beat sounds come back by the same route during the double time beat

10. Return to ordinary reality

11. Record the details of your journey immediately so you don't forget them

Possible issues

1. **Choosing a difficult path:** You can change your entry route as often as you want. When you find one that you are comfortable with, that one should be used consistently.

2. **Can't find the boundary:** This is your route. You control what it looks like, how it feels and how long it takes. 'Talk' yourself through it. You can try using a different route that feels more comfortable. Make the boundary a definite landmark.

3. **Everything is white or dark:** The spirits may be asking you to use all of your senses instead of relying just on sight. Everything you see, touch, smell, hear or just 'know' gives you information. What are your other senses telling you?

4. **You met a spirit but couldn't tell what it was:** This may be a helping spirit, or not. You'll find out in the next journey.

Record your impressions immediately before you forget your experiences. What did your path look like? Describe your path, the colors, the scents, the feeling you had on the path—your spirits—what did they look like, feel like, communicate to you? How did they communicate it to you?

Journey & Journal

Record your impressions immediately before you forget your experiences. Are you keeping updates in your journal? Remember, the information you receive when journeying is often like information you get in a dream—as you return to the beta state of mind much of the information fades and is often ultimately lost. Therefore, be sure to make it a habit to journey and journal immediately afterward.

_____

_____

_____

_____

_____

_____

_____

_____

_____

_____

_____

_____

_____

_____

_____

_____

_____

_____

Exercise 9: Meeting Your Middle World Helping Spirit

The purpose of this exercise is to go to the Middle World and meet a helping spirit. This spirit may be a nature spirit, a spirit of the land or a spirit of a certain place. Other spirits of the Middle World are the elementals such as the fairies, elves, gnomes, nymphs, and divas, to name just a few. These beings are associated with the four elements: earth, water, air and fire and they embody the energy of the element they represent.

Begin the journey by approaching your path or route in your mind. Ask your power animal to go with you. State the intention of the journey "The intention for this journey is to go to the Middle World and meet a helping spirit." Start the drumming CD (20 min track). Follow your route toward the boundary and state the intention of the journey a second time "The intention for this journey is to go to the Middle World and meet a helping spirit." Mentally 'talk' yourself through the boundary (gate or bridge or thicket) and step out into the Middle World. State the intention for the journey for the third time. This keeps you focused on your reason for being there. Because you have been so clear about your intention, one or more spirits will appear to meet you. Ask "Are you here to work with me?" If the figure indicates in some way that it is, ask your power animal if this spirit is a good match for you. If the spirit says "No, I'm not," or your power animal says no, then keep looking. Keep asking for a clear indication that you have found a helping spirit and keep looking for non-verbal signs and body language. Ask them to identify themselves and ask what they would like you to call them. Ask how they would like to work with you. At the recall beat, ask the spirit to return you to the starting point, and come back by the same route.

Preparing to journey to find your Middle World helping spirit:

1. Find a comfortable position so you can relax
2. It helps to have an eye shade to shut out the light

3. Picture your entry point to the Middle World clearly in your mind

4. Start the drumming tape or some other percussion tape (rattle, Tibetan bowls, chanting, etc.) (20 min track)

5. You can ask your power animal to come with you

6. State your intention to find your helping spirit in your mind

7. Picture yourself approaching your route to the Middle World

8. State your intention again while on your route to the Middle World

9. Look ahead to the boundary; Pass through the boundary into a landscape

10. Look around for your helping spirit; Ask your power animal if this spirit is a good match for you

11. When the recall beat sounds thank your helping spirit and ask him/her to take you back to your route home

12. Come back via the same route during the double time beat

13. Return to ordinary reality

14. Record the details of your journey immediately so you don't forget them

Possible issues

1. **You see lots of spirits:** Focus on the spirit that seems to stay with you or that stands out in some way, especially if he/she indicates they are trying to communicate with you. If no one seems to notice you, go further into the Middle World.

2. **You don't see anyone:** Sometimes you have to go to a different landscape to meet someone. Remember that you must use all of your senses. Do you 'feel' as if there is anyone there? Remember that Middle World spirits take many forms.

3. **More than one spirit responds:** If more than one spirit volunteers to help you, that is a good thing. Ask your power

animal to check them all out. Thank them for coming and ask them how they want to work with you.

4. **It takes a long time:** If you are not seeing any spirits or they don't seem to be responding keep repeating the intention of the journey. And relax!

Journey & Journal

Record your impressions immediately before you forget your experiences. Are you keeping updates in your journal? Remember, the information you receive when journeying is often like information you get in a dream—as you return to the beta state of mind much of the information fades and is often ultimately lost. Therefore, be sure to make it a habit to journey and journal immediately afterward.

_____

_____

_____

_____

_____

_____

_____

_____

_____

_____

_____

_____

_____

_____

_____

_____

_____

_____

Exercise 10: Asking Your Middle World Helping Spirit a Question

Before you start to journey set your intention for the journey and define the question you wish to ask. Your intention is to journey to the Middle World and ask your helping spirit a question. The question can be anything you want information on. Questions should be open ended, rather than yes or no questions. *The traditional rule is one question—one journey.* If you ask questions on more than one topic it's difficult to sort out which information goes with which question. The question should also be simple and specific, no 'and/or' phrases.

Example question formats

- What can you tell me about …
- What is my next step regarding …
- How can you help me with …
- What do I need to know about …

After you have defined your question you can prepare to journey

1. Find a comfortable position so you can relax
2. It helps to have an eye shade to shut out the light
3. Picture your route to the Middle World clearly in your mind
4. Ask your power animal to come with you
5. Start the drumming tape or some other percussion tape (rattle, Tibetan bowls, chanting, etc.)
6. State your intention and question in your mind
7. Picture yourself on your path or route
8. Picture the boundary ahead as a gate or bridge or thicket
9. State your intention and question again while approaching the boundary

10. Go into and through the boundary; come out into a garden or landscape

11. Look around for your helping spirit and again state your intention and question

12. Go with your helping spirit as information is presented and your question is answered (10 min or 20 min track)

13. When the recall beat sounds, thank your helping spirit and ask him/her to take you back to the boundary

14. Come back via the same route during the double time beat

15. Return to ordinary reality

16. Record the details of your journey immediately so you don't forget them

Interpreting your journey

What did your helping spirit do when you asked the question? Did you receive information telepathically in your mind or did you 'see' something? What was the 'feel' or energy of the information you received? Did your Middle World spirit take you somewhere and what was the scenario you experienced there? What did you experience through all of your senses?

Journey & Journal

Record your impressions immediately before you forget your experiences. Are you keeping updates in your journal? Remember, the information you receive when journeying is often like information you get in a dream—as you return to the beta state of mind much of the information fades and is often ultimately lost. Therefore, be sure to make it a habit to journey and journal immediately afterward.

_____

_____

_____

_____

Exercise 11: Asking Your Middle World Spirit to Help With a Project

The purpose of this exercise is to ask a nature spirit to help with your garden.

Before you start, set your intention for the journey and define how you will ask the nature spirit for help. Your intention is to journey to the Middle World and ask your helping spirit for help with your garden. So you need to be specific about what you are asking for. Do you want to know the best place to put the garden? What do you intend to plant, vegetables or flowers or both? Are you having problems with pests and need to speak to the insect divas? Or are you asking for the garden fairies to watch over your plants and help them to thrive? All of these are possible. In fact, avid gardeners are most likely doing this subconsciously on a regular basis simply by being very in harmony with the energy of their garden.

Middle World journeys can be done to enlist the aid of the spirits in other projects too. A landscaping or remodeling job can be done with a minimum of disruption. Benevolent spirits can be recruited to watch over a community park or playground. An area damaged by trash and pollution can be brought back into balance and harmony. Middle World spirits want to help us live in harmony with nature because that in turn promotes balance in the universe.

After you have defined your project you can prepare to journey

1. Find a comfortable position so you can relax

2. It helps to have an eye shade to shut out the light

3. Picture your route to the Middle World clearly in your mind

4. Ask your power animal to come with you

5. Start the drumming tape or some other percussion tape (rattle, Tibetan bowls, chanting, etc.)

6. State your intention for the journey in your mind

7. Picture yourself on your path or route to the Middle World

8. Picture the boundary ahead as a gate or bridge or thicket

9. State your intention again while approaching the boundary

10. Go into and through the boundary; come out into a garden or landscape

11. Look around for your helping spirit and again state your intention

12. Go with your helping spirit as information is presented about your project (10 min or 20 min track)

13. When the recall beat sounds, thank your helping spirit and ask him/her to take you back to the boundary

14. Come back via the same route during the double time beat

15. Return to ordinary reality

16. Record the details of your journey immediately so you don't forget them

Interpreting your journey

What did your helping spirit do when you asked the question? Did you receive information telepathically in your mind or did you 'see' something? What was the 'feel' or energy of the information you received? Did your Middle World spirit take you somewhere and what was the scenario you experienced there? What did you experience through all of your senses?

Journey & Journal

Record your impressions immediately before you forget your experiences. Are you keeping updates in your journal? Remember, the information you receive when journeying is often like information you get in a dream—as you return to the beta state of mind much of the information fades and is often ultimately lost. Therefore, be sure to make it a habit to journey and journal immediately afterward.

_____

_____

_____

Exercise 12: Connecting with the spirit of your home

Once you have connected with the spirit of your home and have created a peaceful connection, you can ask your home's spirit to guide you in home improvements, energy balancing, furnishings, even plants. For example: The spirit of our home told me to maintain the emotional and spiritual harmony of our family by representing all four elements, earth, fire, water and air, in the décor of the home and yard. This was very helpful in balancing the energy during the chaotic teenage years. I was also told to work with the garden spirits to maintain the health and vitality of our vegetable garden.

Whether you rent or own you live in a place you call home. Sometimes, if we are lucky, we find a place that resonates with our energy and it is easy to live in harmony with the spirit of that place. Other times we live in a place that never seems to welcome us even though all of the surface features meet our needs and wants.

The purpose of this exercise is to connect with the spirit of your place of residence. This is a Middle World journey but you can take your power animal or teacher with you. Use your route to the Middle World and ask to be taken to the spirit of this place.

Recognize and acknowledge that the spirit has been there a lot longer than you have. Introduce yourself to the spirit and tell it about yourself, whether you are a temporary renter or have purchased the land. Ask the spirit about the history of the land and what you can do to live there in harmony and balance. Are any actions needed to heal the spirit of the land and restore its life force? Do you need to do any maintenance activities to counter other external influences?

After you have set your intention you can prepare to journey

1. Find a comfortable position so you can relax

2. It helps to have an eye shade to shut out the light

3. Picture your route to the Middle World clearly in your mind

4. Ask your power animal to come with you

5. Start the drumming tape or some other percussion tape (rattle, Tibetan bowls, chanting, etc.) (10 min, 20 min or 30 min track)

6. State your intention for the journey in your mind

7. Picture yourself on your path or route to the Middle World

8. Picture the boundary ahead as a gate or bridge or thicket (Whatever you use consistently)

9. State your intention again while approaching the boundary

10. Go into and through the boundary; come out into a garden or landscape

11. Look around for the spirit of your home and again state your intention

12. Ask the spirit of your home your questions

13. When the recall beat sounds, thank the spirit of your home and go back to the boundary

14. Come back via the same route during the double time beat

15. Return to ordinary reality

16. Record the details of your journey immediately so you don't forget them

Interpreting your journey

What did your helping spirit do when you asked the question? Did you receive information telepathically in your mind or did you 'see' something? What was the 'feel' or energy of the information you received? Did your helping spirit take you somewhere and what was the scenario you experienced there? What did you experience through all of your senses?

Journey & Journal

Record your impressions immediately before you forget your experiences. Are you keeping updates in your journal? Remember, the information you receive when journeying is often like information you get in a dream—as you return to the beta state of mind much of the information fades and is often ultimately lost. Therefore, be sure to make it a habit to journey and journal immediately afterward.

_____

_____

_____

_____

_____

_____

_____

_____

_____

_____

_____

_____

_____

_____

_____

_____

_____

_____

_____

_____

_____

_____

_____

_____

_____

Exercise 13: Working with the ancestors

Many shamanic cultures revere and call on their ancestors as their main helping spirits. One of the important factors of working in the Middle World is the ability to go back and heal the ancestral line of physical, emotional, mental and spiritual imbalances. This stops the spiritual tendency for many conditions from being carried forward into future generations.

There is no time in non-ordinary reality so it is possible to travel back to the ancestors to ask for information and guidance. It is also possible to ask for a way to heal the ancestral line for the spiritual aspects of genetic pre-dispositions such as cancer, depression and diabetes. Remember that this is the spiritual aspect of healing which addresses disharmony and imbalance within the ancestral line.

These are Middle World journeys but you can always take a power animal, teacher or Middle World spirit that you trust as your guide.

1. Journey to the ancestors of a place you are interested in to ask about the history of the land and the events that occurred there. Ask the former inhabitants what is needed, if anything, to restore health and vitality to the energy of the place.

   Caution: Do not do this exercise alone at a former battlefield. Do it there only with a group of experienced shamanic practitioners.

2. Journey to your own ancestors to find out when/where a genetic pre-disposition occurred in the ancestral line. Ask to be shown how the DNA was changed and passed down through generations. Ask if the health of the DNA blueprint can be restored through spiritual means and how that can be accomplished.

3. Journey to your own ancestors to find out when/where a family belief or tradition that is no longer serving you first occurred. Ask to be shown the circumstances that prompted

that belief and the purpose it served. Ask what you need to do to change the influence of that belief or tradition in your life today.

4. Ask for healing throughout the ancestral line back to the point of origin. Ask the ancestors if a ceremony or ritual is necessary to clear whatever comes up and what that ceremony consists of.

It may be sufficient to use Morrnah's Ho'Oponopono Prayer (Hawaiian Shaman).

Divine creator, father, mother, son as one … If I, my family, relatives and ancestors have offended you, your family, relatives and ancestors in thoughts, words, deeds and actions from the beginning of our creation to the present, we ask your forgiveness … Let this cleanse, purify, release, cut all the negative memories, blocks, energies and vibrations, and transmute these unwanted energies into pure light … And it is done.

After you have defined your intention you can prepare to journey

1. Find a comfortable position so you can relax

2. It helps to have an eye shade to shut out the light

3. Picture your route to the Middle World clearly in your mind

4. Ask your power animal to come with you

5. Start the drumming tape or some other percussion tape (rattle, Tibetan bowls, chanting, etc.) (10 min, 20 min or 30 min track)

6. State your intention for the journey in your mind

7. Picture yourself on your path or route to the Middle World

8. Picture the boundary ahead as a gate or bridge or thicket (whatever you consistently use)

9. State your intention again while approaching the boundary

10. Go into and through the boundary; come out into a garden or landscape

11. Look around for your ancestor and again state your intention

12. Go with your ancestor as information is presented about your question

13. When the recall beat sounds, thank your ancestor and ask him/her to take you back to the boundary

14. Come back via the same route during the double time beat

15. Return to ordinary reality

16. Record the details of your journey immediately so you don't forget them

Interpreting your journey

What did your ancestor do when you asked the question? Did you receive information telepathically in your mind or did you 'see' something? What was the 'feel' or energy of the information you received? Did your ancestor take you somewhere and what was the scenario you experienced there? What did you experience through all of your senses?

Journey & Journal

Record your impressions immediately before you forget your experiences. Are you keeping updates in your journal? Remember, the information you receive when journeying is often like information you get in a dream—as you return to the beta state of mind much of the information fades and is often ultimately lost. Therefore, be sure to make it a habit to journey and journal immediately afterward.

_____

_____

_____

_____

_____

_____

_____

Exercise 14: Working with the descendents

This is a powerful exercise that can actually influence what we call the "perceptual future."

Since there is no time in non-ordinary reality it is possible to travel forward to consult with our descendents for information and advice. This is a very hopeful approach since the very fact that we have descendents insures the survival of the human race. It gives us the means not only to survive but to thrive in the future in harmony with our environment.

These are Middle World journeys but you can always take a power animal, teacher or Middle World spirit that you trust as your guide.

1. Journey to the descendents at a place you are interested in at a time in the future when all in the environment is in balance and harmony. Ask the spirits how we reached that future. What were the steps that were taken to insure that future? What are the steps we can do today to get started on that path?

2. Journey to the descendents of your ancestral line to find out how to counter possible threats to the integrity and health of your DNA blueprint. How do we pass to our children the greatest probability of health and wellness? What lifestyle changes need to be made now to encourage balance and harmony in the future?

3. Journey to the descendents to find out how health and wellness is maintained in the future. How does healing incorporate all aspects of our beings: physical, emotional, mental, spiritual and energetic? How can we start implementing these healing techniques in our lives today?

After you have defined your intention you can prepare to journey

1. Find a comfortable position so you can relax

2. It helps to have an eye shade to shut out the light

3. Picture your route to the Middle World clearly in your mind

4. Ask your power animal to come with you

5. Start the drumming tape or some other percussion tape (rattle, Tibetan bowls, chanting, etc.) (10 min, 20 min or 30 min track)

6. State your intention for the journey in your mind

7. Picture yourself on your path or route to the Middle World

8. Picture the boundary ahead as a gate or bridge or thicket (whatever you consistently use)

9. State your intention again while approaching the boundary

10. Go into and through the boundary; come out into a garden or landscape

11. Look around for your descendent helping spirit and again state your intention

12. Go with your descendent helping spirit as information is presented about your question

13. When the recall beat sounds, thank your descendent helping spirit and ask him/her to take you back to the boundary

14. Come back via the same route during the double time beat

15. Return to ordinary reality

16. Record the details of your journey immediately so you don't forget them

Interpreting your journey

What did your descendent helping spirit do when you asked the question? Did you receive information telepathically in your mind or did you 'see' something? What was the 'feel' or energy of the information you received? Did your descendent helping spirit take you somewhere and what was the scenario you experienced there? What did you experience through all of your senses?

Journey & Journal

Record your impressions immediately before you forget your experiences. Are you keeping updates in your journal? Remember, the information you receive when journeying is often like information you get in a dream—as you return to the beta state of mind much of the information fades and is often ultimately lost. Therefore, be sure to make it a habit to journey and journal immediately afterward.

_____

_____

_____

_____

_____

_____

_____

_____

_____

_____

_____

_____

_____

_____

_____

_____

_____

_____

_____

_____

_____

_____

_____

_____

_____

Exercise 15: Personal Empowerment

The purpose of this exercise is to examine how the practice of shamanism gives you the power to make the changes you desire in your life.

Shamanism gives you the means to access your own spiritual guidance with the aid of compassionate, helping spirits. Whatever it is you seek, whether information, healing, guidance or the development of your own spirituality, the practice of shamanism gives you the power to fulfill that need for yourself. You no longer require an intermediary to tell you what to do or how to interpret the answers you receive. When you are consistent in your shamanic practice and you have established a relationship with your power animal or teacher, you can rely on the guidance you are given. The key is being consistent, recording your answers and guidance, and developing a deep relationship with your power animal, teachers and guides. The more frequently you journey, the more you will come to "know intuitively" how to interpret the messages you receive and how to act on them.

When you journey today, pay attention to how you have given your power away to other authority figures. Are you too dependent on the expectations and/or opinions of others? Are you afraid that you don't have the ability to find your way? The spirits are here to help us by giving us the means to spiritual guidance.

1. Go to a power animal or teacher and ask to be shown the meaning of empowerment. Pay particular attention to how you have been or can be empowered to act on your own behalf.

2. Go to a power animal or teacher and ask to be shown how you have the power to make a desired change in your life. Ask what your next step is towards your desired goal.

3. Journey to a power animal or teacher and ask to be shown how you give your power away, whether to other people or to an inability to cope with situations. Ask how you can

change this behavior pattern permanently; what is your first step towards this goal?

After you have defined your intention you can prepare to journey

1. Find a comfortable position so you can relax
2. It helps to have an eye shade to shut out the light
3. Picture your route to the Lower or Upper World clearly in your mind
4. Start the drumming tape or some other percussion tape (rattle, Tibetan bowls, chanting, etc.) (10 min, 20 min or 30 min track)
5. State your intention for the journey in your mind
6. Picture yourself on your path or route to the Lower or Upper World
7. Picture the portal or boundary ahead (whatever you consistently use)
8. State your intention again while approaching the portal or boundary
9. Go into and through the tunnel or boundary; come out into a landscape
10. Look around for your power animal or teacher and again state your intention
11. Go with your power animal or teacher as information is presented about your question
12. When the recall beat sounds, thank your helping spirit and ask him/her to take you back to the boundary
13. Come back via the same route during the double time beat
14. Return to ordinary reality
15. Record the details of your journey immediately so you don't forget them

Interpreting your journey

What did your helping spirit do when you asked the question? Did you receive information telepathically in your mind or did you 'see' something? What was the 'feel' or energy of the information you received? Did your helping spirit take you somewhere and what was the scenario you experienced there? What did you experience through all of your senses?

Journey & Journal

Record your impressions immediately before you forget your experiences. Are you keeping updates in your journal? Remember, the information you receive when journeying is often like information you get in a dream—as you return to the beta state of mind much of the information fades and is often ultimately lost. Therefore, be sure to make it a habit to journey and journal immediately afterward.

Exercise 16: To Solve a Problem: Example: A pattern of attracting negative people into my life

The purpose of this exercise is to use the healing power of shamanism to help you recognize this pattern and change how it manifests in your life.

We all have patterns that repeat in our lives that we would like to understand and change. These patterns may include self-destructive behavior, manifesting what is not good for us, and self-sabotage even when we are trying to heal and make changes. Patterns may come from family belief systems that we absorb at an early age, from past life karma that needs to be resolved, or from deeply wounding traumatic experiences, to name just a few sources.

1. The first step in changing a pattern is knowing that it exists.

2. The second step is acknowledging that the basic pattern repeats even if the details differ.

3. The third step is learning to recognize the early signs of the pattern and stop the behavior before it has a negative impact on your life.

When you journey on this issue, be very clear about your intention. You are looking for information on how a negative behavior pattern affects your life and what you can do to change it.

1. Go to a power animal or teacher and ask for lots of examples about how you attract a certain type of person into your life. Ask to be shown how you initiated these manifestations so you can understand your part in the process.

2. Go to a power animal or teacher and ask to be shown how this negative pattern has repeated throughout your life. What are the outcomes of the relationships and how are they similar?

3. Journey to a power animal or teacher and ask to be shown the common signs that the pattern is repeating so you can recognize it in the future. Particularly ask for early warning

signs that can help you avoid manifesting another negative experience.

4. Then journey to ask what the best way to heal the pattern is—ask for details.

After you have defined your intention you can prepare to journey

1. Find a comfortable position so you can relax

2. It helps to have an eye shade to shut out the light

3. Picture your route to the Lower or Upper World clearly in your mind

4. Start the drumming tape or some other percussion tape (rattle, Tibetan bowls, chanting, etc.) (10 min, 20 min or 30 min track)

5. State your intention for the journey in your mind

6. Picture yourself on your path or route to the Lower or Upper World

7. Picture the portal or boundary ahead (whatever you consistently use)

8. State your intention again while approaching the portal or boundary

9. Go into and through the tunnel or boundary; come out into a landscape

10. Look around for your power animal or teacher and again state your intention

11. Go with your power animal or teacher as information is presented about your question

12. When the recall beat sounds, thank your helping spirit and ask him/her to take you back to the boundary

13. Come back via the same route during the double time beat

14. Return to ordinary reality

15. Record the details of your journey immediately so you don't forget them

Interpreting your journey

What did your helping spirit do when you asked the question? Did you receive information telepathically in your mind or did you 'see' something? What was the 'feel' or energy of the information you received? Did your helping spirit take you somewhere and what was the scenario you experienced there? What did you experience through all of your senses?

Journey & Journal

Record your impressions immediately before you forget your experiences. Are you keeping updates in your journal? Remember, the information you receive when journeying is often like information you get in a dream—as you return to the beta state of mind much of the information fades and is often ultimately lost. Therefore, be sure to make it a habit to journey and journal immediately afterward.

_____

_____

_____

_____

_____

_____

_____

_____

_____

_____

_____

_____

_____

_____

Exercise 17: Problem: Changing destructive behavior patterns by understanding the source of the imbalance causing them

The purpose of this exercise is to work with helping spirits to discover the source of a behavior pattern and find out how to heal it.

Destructive behavior patterns can wreak havoc in our lives. We continue to spend too much money, or eat and drink too much, or lie to ourselves and others, even when we know it is a familiar character trait that we would like very much to stop. We may already have tried to change our self-destructive behavior with some success. In Exercise 16 we obtained information about a repeating pattern and how to recognize it. In this exercise we are looking for the source of the behavior pattern and what it has to teach us about ourselves. Patterns may come from family belief systems that we absorb at an early age, from past life karma that needs to be resolved, or from deeply wounding traumatic experiences, to name a few sources. With the help of your power animal or teacher, you can trace the pattern back to its source and find out what healing is needed to change it into a positive influence in your life.

Possible issue: If you are seeing a professional therapist for previous trauma or abuse issues, consult with them before doing these journeys.

When you journey on negative behavior patterns it is helpful to find out how and when the pattern originated. What purpose does it fulfill in your life? How can you heal the original wound to effect permanent change?

1. Go to a power animal or teacher and ask to be shown the original manifestation of the pattern. Ask when and how this occurred and the impact it had on you at that time. Ask to be shown the need or the void that the pattern attempts to address.

2. Go to a power animal or teacher and ask how the impact of the original event can be healed. Can you accomplish this

through your own actions or do you need to find a professional to help you? How do you heal all aspects of the pattern? How do you know when you are done?

After you have defined your intention you can prepare to journey

1. Find a comfortable position so you can relax
2. It helps to have an eye shade to shut out the light
3. Picture your route to the Lower or Upper World clearly in your mind
4. Start the drumming tape or some other percussion tape (rattle, Tibetan bowls, chanting, etc.) (10 min, 20 min or 30 min track)
5. State your intention for the journey in your mind
6. Picture yourself on your path or route to the Lower or Upper World
7. Picture the portal or boundary ahead (whatever you consistently use)
8. State your intention again while approaching the portal or boundary
9. Go into and through the tunnel or boundary; come out into a landscape
10. Look around for your power animal or teacher and again state your intention
11. Go with your power animal or teacher as information is presented about your question
12. When the recall beat sounds, thank your helping spirit and ask him/her to take you back to the boundary
13. Come back via the same route during the double time beat
14. Return to ordinary reality
15. Record the details of your journey immediately so you don't forget them

Interpreting your journey

What did your helping spirit do when you asked the question? Did you receive information telepathically in your mind or did you 'see' something? What was the 'feel' or energy of the information you received? Did your helping spirit take you somewhere and what was the scenario you experienced there? What did you experience through all of your senses?

Journey & Journal

Record your impressions immediately before you forget your experiences. Are you keeping updates in your journal? Remember, the information you receive when journeying is often like information you get in a dream—as you return to the beta state of mind much of the information fades and is often ultimately lost. Therefore, be sure to make it a habit to journey and journal immediately afterward.

_____

_____

_____

_____

_____

_____

_____

_____

_____

_____

_____

_____

_____

_____

_____

_____

Exercise 18: To Solve a Problem: Example: How do I know if a new relationship is good for me?

The purpose of this exercise is to ask for information about entering into a new relationship.

New relationships can be scary at the best of times. Most of us have felt the pain of severing a relationship when it just didn't work out. Both people and circumstances change over time and differences can become unbearable. So we all try to determine in advance whether this new person in our life is truly our soul mate. The problem is that in this reality we are limited to information we gather only through our physical senses or that nebulous thing called intuition.

And many of us no longer trust that we are receiving the correct information or that we are interpreting the signs accurately. The shamanic journey gives us access to information beyond our senses. Our helping spirits give us insights and understanding into issues we may be feeling but cannot put into words. This information reinforces what our own inner truth is trying to tell us and validates what we already know. There are many aspects to a relationship that can be examined in this manner.

Remember that the spirits rarely give us a yes/no, black or white answer to our question. It is important to ask open ended questions to elicit more information so we can make informed decisions. Be aware of everything in the journey—it is all part of the answer. You interpret the answer by figuring out what the metaphors, symbols and examples mean to you.

1. Go to a power animal or teacher and ask "What do I need to know about entering into a relationship with this person? If the answer is not clear, keep asking for more information and more examples until you are satisfied.

2. Go to a power animal or teacher and ask how a relationship with this person will affect your life. You may get insights that will surprise you.

After you have defined your intention you can prepare to journey

1. Find a comfortable position so you can relax
2. It helps to have an eye shade to shut out the light
3. Picture your route to the Lower or Upper World clearly in your mind
4. Start the drumming tape or some other percussion tape (rattle, Tibetan bowls, chanting, etc.) (10 min, 20 min or 30 min track)
5. State your intention for the journey in your mind
6. Picture yourself on your path or route to the Lower or Upper World
7. Picture the portal or boundary ahead (whatever you consistently use)
8. State your intention again while approaching the portal or boundary
9. Go into and through the tunnel or boundary; come out into a landscape
10. Look around for your power animal or teacher and again state your intention
11. Go with your power animal or teacher as information is presented about your question
12. When the recall beat sounds, thank your helping spirit and ask him/her to take you back to the boundary
13. Come back via the same route during the double time beat
14. Return to ordinary reality
15. Record the details of your journey immediately so you don't forget them

Interpreting your journey

What did your helping spirit do when you asked the question? Did you receive information telepathically in your mind or did you 'see' something? What was the 'feel' or energy of the information you

received? Did your helping spirit take you somewhere and what was the scenario you experienced there? What did you experience through all of your senses?

Journey & Journal

Record your impressions immediately before you forget your experiences. Are you keeping updates in your journal? Remember, the information you receive when journeying is often like information you get in a dream—as you return to the beta state of mind much of the information fades and is often ultimately lost. Therefore, be sure to make it a habit to journey and journal immediately afterward.

_____

_____

_____

_____

_____

_____

_____

_____

_____

_____

_____

_____

_____

_____

_____

_____

_____

_____

_____

Exercise 19: To Solve a Problem: Example: How do I cope with the issues of divorce or separation

The purpose of this exercise is to ask for guidance and healing in dealing with the emotional pain of separation or divorce.

Just as new relationships can be terrifying, the experience of separation and divorce can be devastating. Indeed, the possibility of divorce is what makes most of us so reluctant to open up again. How do you heal the feelings of inadequacy and fear that can prevent you from moving forward? How do you recover from emotional pain and restore peace and serenity to your life? Can you find happiness, balance and harmony during and after a process that makes you feel like a failure? Shamanism addresses the spiritual aspect of healing. Your wounded spirit will find solace and support from your power animals and teachers in non-ordinary reality. They will give you ways to incorporate this healing back into your daily life. There is life after divorce and it will become worth living again.

You can ask the spirits for a healing at any time and they are happy to oblige. Just as we strive to live in happiness and fulfillment, the spiritual realm strives to promote balance and harmony in the whole of existence. Since we are all connected, healing the individual also heals the whole.

1. Go to a power animal or teacher and ask for a healing. You will receive exactly what you need at this point in time. This journey may be repeated as often as you like.

2. Go to a power animal or teacher and ask how to soothe the emotional pain that is affecting your daily life. Ask for ways to restore balance, peace and serenity.

After you have defined your intention you can prepare to journey

1. Find a comfortable position so you can relax

2. It helps to have an eye shade to shut out the light

3. Picture your route to the Lower or Upper World clearly in your mind

4. Start the drumming tape or some other percussion tape (rattle, Tibetan bowls, chanting, etc.) (10 min, 20 min or 30 min track)

5. State your intention for the journey in your mind

6. Picture yourself on your path or route to the Lower or Upper World

7. Picture the portal or boundary ahead (whatever you consistently use)

8. State your intention again while approaching the portal or boundary

9. Go into and through the tunnel or boundary; come out into a landscape

10. Look around for your power animal or teacher and again state your intention

11. Go with your power animal or teacher as information is presented about your question

12. When the recall beat sounds, thank your helping spirit and ask him / her to take you back to the boundary

13. Come back via the same route during the double time beat

14. Return to ordinary reality

15. Record the details of your journey immediately so you don't forget them

Interpreting your journey

What did your helping spirit do when you asked the question? Did you receive information telepathically in your mind or did you 'see' something? What was the 'feel' or energy of the information you received? Did your helping spirit take you somewhere and what was the scenario you experienced there? What did you experience through all of your senses?

Journey & Journal

Record your impressions immediately before you forget your experiences. Are you keeping updates in your journal? Remember, the information you receive when journeying is often like information you get in a dream—as you return to the beta state of mind much of the information fades and is often ultimately lost. Therefore, be sure to make it a habit to journey and journal immediately afterward.

_____

_____

_____

_____

_____

_____

_____

_____

_____

_____

_____

_____

_____

_____

_____

_____

_____

_____

_____

_____

_____

_____

_____

_____

Exercise 20: To Solve a Problem: Example: How do I resolve family conflict?

The purpose of this exercise is to ask for information and guidance in dealing with conflict.

Since we are all individuals evolving at our own pace, conflict is a fact of life. It's pretty unrealistic to think that we are all going to agree on everything. Sometimes the most we can hope for is that we agree to disagree. This is particularly hard in family or career situations where we need to interact on an on-going basis. At the least it is uncomfortable. Taken to extremes it can cause family rifts and destroy careers. Shamanism can help resolve conflict by giving us insight and understanding of the underlying beliefs and issues involved. It can help us perceive different points of view and relate to the feelings of others. We cannot journey for someone else, nor can we ask the spirits to change another's behavior. But we can ask to understand why they have a particular opinion. We can also ask what we need to do to change the energy involved in the conflict to promote well-being for all concerned.

In your journeys concerning conflict resolution be sure to approach it as your issue. What do you need to do? What do you need to change? How can you understand the other person's viewpoint? What aspects of the situation were you not aware of?

1. Go to a power animal or teacher and ask for information about all aspects of a conflict situation. Ask to be shown the source of the other's point of view. Ask for understanding of the issues involved.

2. Go to a power animal or teacher and ask how you can change your approach or response to the situation. Ask for guidance on how to change the energy of the conflict to promote acceptance and harmony.

After you have defined your intention you can prepare to journey

1. Find a comfortable position so you can relax

2. It helps to have an eye shade to shut out the light

3. Picture your route to the Lower or Upper World clearly in your mind

4. Start the drumming tape or some other percussion tape (rattle, Tibetan bowls, chanting, etc.) (10 min, 20 min or 30 min track)

5. State your intention for the journey in your mind

6. Picture yourself on your path or route to the Lower or Upper World

7. Picture the portal or boundary ahead (whatever you consistently use)

8. State your intention again while approaching the portal or boundary

9. Go into and through the tunnel or boundary; come out into a landscape

10. Look around for your power animal or teacher and again state your intention

11. Go with your power animal or teacher as information is presented about your question

12. When the recall beat sounds, thank your helping spirit and ask him/her to take you back to the boundary

13. Come back via the same route during the double time beat

14. Return to ordinary reality

15. Record the details of your journey immediately so you don't forget them

Interpreting your journey

What did your helping spirit do when you asked the question? Did you receive information telepathically in your mind or did you 'see' something? What was the 'feel' or energy of the information you received? Did your helping spirit take you somewhere and what was the scenario you experienced there? What did you experience through all of your senses?

Journey & Journal

Record your impressions immediately before you forget your experiences. Are you keeping updates in your journal? Remember, the information you receive when journeying is often like information you get in a dream—as you return to the beta state of mind much of the information fades and is often ultimately lost. Therefore, be sure to make it a habit to journey and journal immediately afterward.

_____

_____

_____

_____

_____

_____

_____

_____

_____

_____

_____

_____

_____

_____

_____

_____

_____

_____

_____

_____

_____

_____

_____

_____

_____

Exercise 21: To Solve a Problem: Example: How do I cope with feeling alone and isolated?

The purpose of this exercise is to ask for support and guidance after moving to a new community.

Moving to a new location can be fun and exciting, but also stressful and challenging. It usually involves a new work environment along with the chaos of setting up a new living space. If you are doing this alone, it is normal to feel alone and isolated, at least for a while. If you are not alone, family members may be experiencing these feelings and have difficulty fitting into peer groups at school and work. Relationships within the family may be strained as well. Since things and events usually manifest on the spiritual plane before we experience them in this reality, now it is very important to establish harmony and balance emotionally and spiritually. The best and easiest way to do this is to work with your helping spirits, asking for support and guidance in making new connections at work and in the community. This can be a very good way to make a new start by changing old behavior patterns and old belief systems. Your helping spirits are eager to support you in making the most of this opportunity.

In your journeys concerning aloneness and isolation, be sure to approach it as your issue. What do you need to do? What do you need to change? How can you understand the other person's viewpoint? What aspects of the situation were you not aware of?

1. Go to a power animal or teacher and ask for information about all aspects of the isolating situation. Ask to be shown the source of the other family member's point of view. Ask for understanding of the issues involved.

2. Go to a power animal or teacher and ask how you can change your approach or response to the situation. Ask for guidance on how to change the energy of the situation to promote acceptance and harmony.

After you have defined your intention you can prepare to journey

1. Find a comfortable position so you can relax
2. It helps to have an eye shade to shut out the light
3. Picture your route to the Lower or Upper World clearly in your mind
4. Start the drumming tape or some other percussion tape (rattle, Tibetan bowls, chanting, etc.) (10 min, 20 min or 30 min track)
5. State your intention for the journey in your mind
6. Picture yourself on your path or route to the Lower or Upper World
7. Picture the portal or boundary ahead (whatever you consistently use)
8. State your intention again while approaching the portal or boundary
9. Go into and through the tunnel or boundary; come out into a landscape
10. Look around for your power animal or teacher and again state your intention
11. Go with your power animal or teacher as information is presented about your question
12. When the recall beat sounds, thank your helping spirit and ask him/her to take you back to the boundary
13. Come back via the same route during the double time beat
14. Return to ordinary reality
15. Record the details of your journey immediately so you don't forget them

Interpreting your journey

What did your helping spirit do when you asked the question? Did you receive information telepathically in your mind or did you 'see' something? What was the 'feel' or energy of the information you

received? Did your helping spirit take you somewhere and what was the scenario you experienced there? What did you experience through all of your senses?

Journey & Journal

Record your impressions immediately before you forget your experiences. Are you keeping updates in your journal? Remember, the information you receive when journeying is often like information you get in a dream—as you return to the beta state of mind much of the information fades and is often ultimately lost. Therefore, be sure to make it a habit to journey and journal immediately afterward.

_____

_____

_____

_____

_____

_____

_____

_____

_____

_____

_____

_____

_____

_____

_____

_____

_____

_____

_____

_____

Exercise 22: To Solve a Problem:
Example: How do I keep my relationship
with my partner fresh and exciting?

The purpose of this exercise is to ask for information and guidance in maintaining excitement in a long-standing relationship.

Mature long-standing relationships can be very stabilizing and comfortable, but the risk is that they can also become complacent and boring. It is too easy to take the other person for granted and fall into habits that are expected and anticipated. As time goes on, it becomes difficult to keep the relationship fresh and exciting. You can use the power of shamanic journeying to explore ways to spice up the relationship. You can also ask your power animal or teacher to help you address any issues that may be affecting you and your partner. The more information and guidance you have, the better you can change the energy around the situation. Remember that you must address this as your issue. The best would be if both you and your partner can journey together about any issues and resolve them together, achieving balance and harmony. Relationships have physical, emotional and spiritual aspects just as individuals do, and the spirits can help us maintain the energy in all of them.

The spirits love to help us achieve the best connections we can. Ask your power animal or teacher what you need to do. What do you need to change? How can you understand the energy of the relationship? What aspects of the situation were you not aware of?

1. Go to a power animal or teacher and ask for information about all aspects of the relationship. Ask to be shown how the excitement you generate manifests in the relationship.

2. Go to a power animal or teacher and ask how you can change your approach or response to the situation. Ask for understanding of the issues involved. Ask for guidance on how to change the energy of the situation to promote acceptance and harmony.

After you have defined your intention you can prepare to journey

1. Find a comfortable position so you can relax

2. It helps to have an eye shade to shut out the light

3. Picture your route to the Lower or Upper World clearly in your mind

4. Start the drumming tape or some other percussion tape (rattle, Tibetan bowls, chanting, etc.) (10 min, 20 min or 30 min track)

5. State your intention for the journey in your mind

6. Picture yourself on your path or route to the Lower or Upper World

7. Picture the portal or boundary ahead (whatever you consistently use)

8. State your intention again while approaching the portal or boundary

9. Go into and through the tunnel or boundary; come out into a landscape

10. Look around for your power animal or teacher and again state your intention

11. Go with your power animal or teacher as information is presented about your question

12. When the recall beat sounds, thank your helping spirit and ask him/her to take you back to the boundary

13. Come back via the same route during the double time beat

14. Return to ordinary reality

15. Record the details of your journey immediately so you don't forget them

Interpreting your journey

What did your helping spirit do when you asked the question? Did you receive information telepathically in your mind or did you 'see' something? What was the 'feel' or energy of the information you

received? Did your helping spirit take you somewhere and what was the scenario you experienced there? What did you experience through all of your senses?

Journey & Journal

Record your impressions immediately before you forget your experiences. Are you keeping updates in your journal? Remember, the information you receive when journeying is often like information you get in a dream—as you return to the beta state of mind much of the information fades and is often ultimately lost. Therefore, be sure to make it a habit to journey and journal immediately afterward.

_____

_____

_____

_____

_____

_____

_____

_____

_____

_____

_____

_____

_____

_____

_____

_____

_____

_____

_____

_____

Exercise 23: To Solve a Problem: Example: How do I let go of negative feelings after divorce?

The purpose of this exercise is to ask for healing and guidance in moving on after divorce.

Breaking up any kind of relationship can challenge everything we feel about ourselves and our former partner. One of the most devastating and damaging effects of dissolving a relationship is feeling and possibly dwelling on the negative emotions of anger, bitterness, hate, regret, etc. These negative emotions can take over your life, preventing you from moving forward and making it seem impossible to find happiness, peace and serenity. Not only does this negativity corrode your own outlook, it affects everyone else around you, creating an environment in which it is very hard to heal and move on. While it is extremely difficult for you to rise above this on your own, fortunately you have spirits you can call on to help you heal the pain and helplessness you experience. Journeying to your helping spirits will help you regain control of your emotions and your life. You can ask for options for healing and for guidance in changing the energy of the situation.

Our spirits love to help us heal and achieve happiness and serenity. Remember that you are journeying only for your situation, not to change anyone else. Ask your power animal or teacher what you need to do. What do you need to change? How can you understand the underlying issues causing the negative feelings?

1. Go to a power animal or teacher and ask for a healing. Ask to be shown how the healing will help you move forward.

2. Go to a power animal or teacher and ask to be shown how the negative feelings are hurting you and impeding your ability to find peace and happiness. Ask to be shown how you can change your perspective and attitude.

After you have defined your intention you can prepare to journey

1. Find a comfortable position so you can relax

2. It helps to have an eye shade to shut out the light

3. Picture your route to the Lower or Upper World clearly in your mind

4. Start the drumming tape or some other percussion tape (rattle, Tibetan bowls, chanting, etc.) (10 min, 20 min or 30 min track)

5. State your intention for the journey in your mind

6. Picture yourself on your path or route to the Lower or Upper World

7. Picture the portal or boundary ahead (whatever you consistently use)

8. State your intention again while approaching the portal or boundary

9. Go into and through the tunnel or boundary; come out into a landscape

10. Look around for your power animal or teacher and again state your intention

11. Go with your power animal or teacher as information is presented about your question

12. When the recall beat sounds, thank your helping spirit and ask him/her to take you back to the boundary

13. Come back via the same route during the double time beat

14. Return to ordinary reality

15. Record the details of your journey immediately so you don't forget them

Interpreting your journey

What did your helping spirit do when you asked the question? Did you receive information telepathically in your mind or did you 'see' something? What was the 'feel' or energy of the information you received? Did your helping spirit take you somewhere and what was the scenario you experienced there? What did you experience through all of your senses?

Journey & Journal

Record your impressions immediately before you forget your experiences. Are you keeping updates in your journal? Remember, the information you receive when journeying is often like information you get in a dream—as you return to the beta state of mind much of the information fades and is often ultimately lost. Therefore, be sure to make it a habit to journey and journal immediately afterward.

_____

_____

_____

_____

_____

_____

_____

_____

_____

_____

_____

_____

_____

_____

_____

_____

_____

_____

_____

_____

_____

_____

_____

_____

_____

Exercise 24: To Solve a Problem: Example: How do I be a GREAT step-parent?

The purpose of this exercise is to ask for support and guidance in being a step-parent.

Starting a new relationship is both fun and challenging. When you add children into the mix it can become more than challenging, it can be downright scary. Being a step-parent is one of the most difficult jobs on the planet. It can be almost impossible to achieve the right balance of love, support, discipline and accountability. This is when you need all of the support you can get, from your partner and from the spirits. You can use the power of shamanic journeying to ask for guidance in setting the right environment for balance and harmony in your home. And you can continue to ask for support and guidance as events and issues arise. Remember that situations change as children go through phases and that you can only journey for yourself, not to change others. The objective is to be the best that you can be, and set the example for everyone else in the home. The spirits can help you do this with love, guidance and support when you need it the most.

When you journey, ask for a power animal or teacher who will be dedicated to helping you with this situation on an on-going basis. You can have many power animals and teachers and it is not unusual to have one you go to for just one function.

1. Ask for a power animal or teacher that will be dedicated to helping you with this situation. Ask how that spirit would like you to work with them. How are they going to support you in creating balance and harmony within the family?

2. As situations and issues arise go to your helping spirit and ask for support and guidance in how to handle the energy of the situation. What is the appropriate action or reaction for the good of all concerned?

After you have defined your intention you can prepare to journey

1. Find a comfortable position so you can relax

2. It helps to have an eye shade to shut out the light

3. Picture your route to the Lower or Upper World clearly in your mind

4. Start the drumming tape or some other percussion tape (rattle, Tibetan bowls, chanting, etc.) (10 min, 20 min or 30 min track)

5. State your intention for the journey in your mind

6. Picture yourself on your path or route to the Lower or Upper World

7. Picture the portal or boundary ahead (whatever you consistently use)

8. State your intention again while approaching the portal or boundary

9. Go into and through the tunnel or boundary; come out into a landscape

10. Look around for your power animal or teacher and again state your intention

11. Go with your power animal or teacher as information is presented about your question

12. When the recall beat sounds, thank your helping spirit and ask him/her to take you back to the boundary

13. Come back via the same route during the double time beat

14. Return to ordinary reality

15. Record the details of your journey immediately so you don't forget them

Interpreting your journey

What did your helping spirit do when you asked the question? Did you receive information telepathically in your mind or did you 'see' something? What was the 'feel' or energy of the information you received? Did your helping spirit take you somewhere and what was the scenario you experienced there? What did you experience through all of your senses?

Journey & Journal

Record your impressions immediately before you forget your experiences. Are you keeping updates in your journal? Remember, the information you receive when journeying is often like information you get in a dream—as you return to the beta state of mind much of the information fades and is often ultimately lost. Therefore, be sure to make it a habit to journey and journal immediately afterward.

_____

_____

_____

_____

_____

_____

_____

_____

_____

_____

_____

_____

_____

_____

_____

_____

_____

_____

_____

_____

_____

_____

_____

Exercise 25: To Solve a Problem: Example: How do I help a challenged child?

The purpose of this exercise is to ask for support and guidance in helping a challenged child.

If your child is challenged physically, mentally or emotionally, it places great demands on your time and energy. It is extremely difficult to balance priorities, especially when other children are also involved. Even when you have explored all of the conventional options, you may feel as if there is still more that you can and should be doing. How can you juggle all of these responsibilities for the good of all concerned? How can you truly know that you have explored all of the options available to you? The spirits can give you insights into conventional and alternative healing and developmental methods that fit well into your family's lifestyle. And on a deeper level the power of the shamanic journey can give you the spiritual support you need to maintain your own balance and strength. In this way you are giving to your family from a place of harmony and joy, instead of depleting your energy until you endanger your own health and well-being. Enhancing your own physical, emotional and spiritual strength and health is the best way to help your entire family, including your child with challenges.

When you journey, ask for a power animal or teacher who will be dedicated to helping you with this situation on an on-going basis. You can have many power animals and teachers and it is not unusual to have one you go to for just one function.

1. Ask for a power animal or teacher that will be dedicated to helping you with this situation. Ask how that spirit would like you to work with them. How are they going to support you in creating balance, health and harmony within the family?

2. As situations and issues arise go to your helping spirit and ask for support and guidance in how to handle the energy of the situation. What is the appropriate action or reaction for the good of all concerned?

After you have defined your intention you can prepare to journey

1. Find a comfortable position so you can relax

2. It helps to have an eye shade to shut out the light

3. Picture your route to the Lower or Upper World clearly in your mind

4. Start the drumming tape or some other percussion tape (rattle, Tibetan bowls, chanting, etc.) (10 min, 20 min or 30 min track)

5. State your intention for the journey in your mind

6. Picture yourself on your path or route to the Lower or Upper World

7. Picture the portal or boundary ahead (whatever you consistently use)

8. State your intention again while approaching the portal or boundary

9. Go into and through the tunnel or boundary; come out into a landscape

10. Look around for your power animal or teacher and again state your intention

11. Go with your power animal or teacher as information is presented about your question

12. When the recall beat sounds, thank your helping spirit and ask him/her to take you back to the boundary

13. Come back via the same route during the double time beat

14. Return to ordinary reality

15. Record the details of your journey immediately so you don't forget them

Interpreting your journey

What did your helping spirit do when you asked the question? Did you receive information telepathically in your mind or did you 'see' something? What was the 'feel' or energy of the information you

received? Did your helping spirit take you somewhere and what was the scenario you experienced there? What did you experience through all of your senses?

Journey & Journal

Record your impressions immediately before you forget your experiences. Are you keeping updates in your journal? Remember, the information you receive when journeying is often like information you get in a dream—as you return to the beta state of mind much of the information fades and is often ultimately lost. Therefore, be sure to make it a habit to journey and journal immediately afterward.

_____

_____

_____

_____

_____

_____

_____

_____

_____

_____

_____

_____

_____

_____

_____

_____

_____

_____

_____

_____

_____

Exercise 26: To Solve a Problem: Example: How do I help a child with behavioral issues?

The purpose of this exercise is to ask for support and guidance in helping a child with behavioral issues.

Behavioral issues can include many scenarios from peer pressure to bullying. If your child is having trouble with peer relationships you may be feeling very helpless in trying to be supportive, yet holding them accountable for their own behavior. While you cannot journey to directly change your child's behavior, you can do a journey to ask a power animal to volunteer to come and help with the situation. You can also use the power of shamanic journeying to ask the spirits for advice in how you can effectively support and guide your child. Be prepared for insights into how you can change your own behavior patterns and how that can influence the energy of the situation. As you achieve balance, harmony and strength, this will be reflected in your child.

When you journey, ask for a power animal or teacher who will be dedicated to helping you with this situation on an on-going basis. You can also ask for a power animal to come and help your child not only cope, but thrive.

1. Ask for a power animal or teacher that will be dedicated to helping you with this situation. Ask how that spirit would like you to work with them. Ask for a power animal to volunteer to come and help your child, supporting them and protecting them.

2. As situations and issues arise go to your helping spirit and ask for support and guidance in how to handle the energy of the situation. What is the appropriate action or reaction for the good of all concerned? How can you change your behavior patterns to help your child?

After you have defined your intention you can prepare to journey

1. Find a comfortable position so you can relax
2. It helps to have an eye shade to shut out the light

3. Picture your route to the Lower or Upper World clearly in your mind

4. Start the drumming tape or some other percussion tape (rattle, Tibetan bowls, chanting, etc.) (10 min, 20 min or 30 min track)

5. State your intention for the journey in your mind

6. Picture yourself on your path or route to the Lower or Upper World

7. Picture the portal or boundary ahead (whatever you consistently use)

8. State your intention again while approaching the portal or boundary

9. Go into and through the tunnel or boundary; come out into a landscape

10. Look around for your power animal or teacher and again state your intention

11. Go with your power animal or teacher as information is presented about your question

12. When the recall beat sounds, thank your helping spirit and ask him/her to take you back to the boundary

13. Come back via the same route during the double time beat

14. Return to ordinary reality

15. Record the details of your journey immediately so you don't forget them

Interpreting your journey

What did your helping spirit do when you asked the question? Did you receive information telepathically in your mind or did you 'see' something? What was the 'feel' or energy of the information you received? Did your helping spirit take you somewhere and what was the scenario you experienced there? What did you experience through all of your senses?

Journey & Journal

Record your impressions immediately before you forget your experiences. Are you keeping updates in your journal? Remember, the information you receive when journeying is often like information you get in a dream—as you return to the beta state of mind much of the information fades and is often ultimately lost. Therefore, be sure to make it a habit to journey and journal immediately afterward.

_____

_____

_____

_____

_____

_____

_____

_____

_____

_____

_____

_____

_____

_____

_____

_____

_____

_____

_____

_____

_____

_____

Exercise 27: To Solve a Problem: Example: How do I help aging parents?

The purpose of this exercise is to ask for support and guidance in helping aging parents.

When the child becomes the caregiver, it can be a difficult situation for everyone involved. Primary considerations of health and safety can conflict with your parent's desires for independence and autonomy. Relationships can become strained as decisions have to be made, whether they are popular or not. The situation can become even more complex when other siblings are also involved. Focusing on the spiritual aspects of the situation can help to bring balance and harmony to all concerned. By using the power of the shamanic journey, you can gain access to all of the options available to solve conflicting priorities. The spirits can help with healing, support and guidance and love to be asked to do so.

When you journey today remember to ask for assistance only from your point of view as you cannot ask to change others. How can you maintain your personal power yet be considerate of the wishes of others? How can you continue to approach a difficult situation with love and caring?

1. Ask your power animal or teacher to show you the options available as you deal with conflicting priorities. How are the spirits going to support you in creating balance, health and harmony within the family?

2. As situations and issues arise go to your helping spirits and ask for support and guidance in how to handle the energy of the situation. What is the appropriate action or reaction for the good of all concerned?

After you have defined your intention you can prepare to journey

1. Find a comfortable position so you can relax

2. It helps to have an eye shade to shut out the light

3. Picture your route to the Lower or Upper World clearly in your mind

4. Start the drumming tape or some other percussion tape (rattle, Tibetan bowls, chanting, etc.) (10 min, 20 min or 30 min track)

5. State your intention for the journey in your mind

6. Picture yourself on your path or route to the Lower or Upper World

7. Picture the portal or boundary ahead (whatever you consistently use)

8. State your intention again while approaching the portal or boundary

9. Go into and through the tunnel or boundary; come out into a landscape

10. Look around for your power animal or teacher and again state your intention

11. Go with your power animal or teacher as information is presented about your question

12. When the recall beat sounds, thank your helping spirit and ask him/her to take you back to the boundary

13. Come back via the same route during the double time beat

14. Return to ordinary reality

15. Record the details of your journey immediately so you don't forget them

Interpreting your journey

What did your helping spirit do when you asked the question? Did you receive information telepathically in your mind or did you 'see' something? What was the 'feel' or energy of the information you received? Did your helping spirit take you somewhere and what was the scenario you experienced there? What did you experience through all of your senses?

Journey & Journal

Record your impressions immediately before you forget your experiences. Are you keeping updates in your journal? Remember, the information you receive when journeying is often like information you get in a dream—as you return to the beta state of mind much of the information fades and is often ultimately lost. Therefore, be sure to make it a habit to journey and journal immediately afterward.

_____

_____

_____

_____

_____

_____

_____

_____

_____

_____

_____

_____

_____

_____

_____

_____

_____

_____

_____

_____

_____

_____

_____

Exercise 28: To Solve a Problem:
Example: How do I get a job?

The purpose of this exercise is to ask for information and guidance in getting a job or finding my life's work.

Being laid off from a job or unable to work for any reason can be a stressful time in anyone's life. Many of us struggle to find work that is meaningful and fulfilling, but still pays the bills. During economic recessions with periods of high unemployment, we may feel desperate enough to accept any position that is offered, hoping to improve our situation at a later time. That's assuming that we even make it through an interview. Resulting impacts can include loss of self esteem, putting our dreams and aspirations on hold, and feeling limited and powerless as we contemplate our future. Working with your helping spirits will not only restore your sense of personal power, it will give you practical steps to regain control of your destiny. Shamanism can help you identify your strengths and abilities and give you practical guidance on how to market these. It can give you insight into what your perfect work situation looks and feels like so you can plan how to manifest it.

In your journeys concentrate on how it feels to be doing the work you love and are really good at. Your power animals and teachers can show you limitless possibilities and give you practical steps on how to get there.

1. Go to a power animal or teacher and ask for information about where you should be putting your energy in looking for work. Are conventional means going to produce results or do you need to investigate other methods? What are these unconventional approaches and how do you apply them?

2. Go to a power animal or teacher and ask how you can market yourself to emphasize your strengths and abilities. Ask how to set up a plan to reach your goal. Ask "What is my next step and how do I do this?" You can repeat this journey as often as necessary.

After you have defined your intention you can prepare to journey

1. Find a comfortable position so you can relax

2. It helps to have an eye shade to shut out the light

3. Picture your route to the Lower or Upper World clearly in your mind

4. Start the drumming tape or some other percussion tape (rattle, Tibetan bowls, chanting, etc.) (10 min, 20 min or 30 min track)

5. State your intention for the journey in your mind

6. Picture yourself on your path or route to the Lower or Upper World

7. Picture the portal or boundary ahead (whatever you consistently use)

8. State your intention again while approaching the portal or boundary

9. Go into and through the tunnel or boundary; come out into a landscape

10. Look around for your power animal or teacher and again state your intention

11. Go with your power animal or teacher as information is presented about your question

12. When the recall beat sounds, thank your helping spirit and ask him/her to take you back to the boundary

13. Come back via the same route during the double time beat

14. Return to ordinary reality

15. Record the details of your journey immediately so you don't forget them

Interpreting your journey

What did your helping spirit do when you asked the question? Did you receive information telepathically in your mind or did you 'see' something? What was the 'feel' or energy of the information you

received? Did your helping spirit take you somewhere and what was the scenario you experienced there? What did you experience through all of your senses?

Journey & Journal

Record your impressions immediately before you forget your experiences. Are you keeping updates in your journal? Remember, the information you receive when journeying is often like information you get in a dream—as you return to the beta state of mind much of the information fades and is often ultimately lost. Therefore, be sure to make it a habit to journey and journal immediately afterward.

_____

_____

_____

_____

_____

_____

_____

_____

_____

_____

_____

_____

_____

_____

_____

_____

_____

_____

_____

_____

Exercise 29: To Solve a Problem: Example: How do I work with money to my best advantage?

The purpose of this exercise is to ask for information and guidance in managing money or finding new sources of income.

It seems like we never have enough, whether its money, time or energy. Usually we feel that if we just had enough money to go around, all of our problems would be solved. We feel this way even though we know that it is not true. Money does not automatically bring happiness or fulfillment. But it can take care of the basics of food, clothing and shelter, and provide the framework for opportunity, freedom and self-expression. The key is to think of money as a universal resource that is not an end of a process, but a means to achieving a goal. It comes in, we allocate it to a particular purpose, and it goes back out again. Shamanism is a spiritual practice that restores and maintains balance and harmony. This applies to all forms of energy, including money. You can use the principles and techniques of shamanism to understand the flow of money and how to use it to your best advantage. Understanding the energy of money will help you attract it and direct it in a conscious way.

It is tempting to think of money in terms of good or bad, plenty or lack. In your journeys about money, look at it as neutral energy with a natural ebb and flow. Remember the saying, "Where the energy goes, the money follows." Pay attention to where your energy is going.

1. Go to a power animal or teacher and ask for information about the nature of money. How can you understand it and direct it to achieve a goal? How do you currently use the money you have and how can you improve on this?

2. Go to a power animal or teacher and ask how you can attract more money. Ask if money is what you really need or is it some other resource you have been neglecting. You can repeat this journey as often as necessary.

After you have defined your intention you can prepare to journey

1. Find a comfortable position so you can relax

2. It helps to have an eye shade to shut out the light

3. Picture your route to the Lower or Upper World clearly in your mind

4. Start the drumming tape or some other percussion tape (rattle, Tibetan bowls, chanting, etc.) (10 min, 20 min or 30 min track)

5. State your intention for the journey in your mind

6. Picture yourself on your path or route to the Lower or Upper World

7. Picture the portal or boundary ahead (whatever you consistently use)

8. State your intention again while approaching the portal or boundary

9. Go into and through the tunnel or boundary; come out into a landscape

10. Look around for your power animal or teacher and again state your intention

11. Go with your power animal or teacher as information is presented about your question

12. When the recall beat sounds, thank your helping spirit and ask him/her to take you back to the boundary

13. Come back via the same route during the double time beat

14. Return to ordinary reality

15. Record the details of your journey immediately so you don't forget them

Interpreting your journey

What did your helping spirit do when you asked the question? Did you receive information telepathically in your mind or did you 'see' something? What was the 'feel' or energy of the information you

received? Did your helping spirit take you somewhere and what was the scenario you experienced there? What did you experience through all of your senses?

Journey & Journal

Record your impressions immediately before you forget your experiences. Are you keeping updates in your journal? Remember, the information you receive when journeying is often like information you get in a dream—as you return to the beta state of mind much of the information fades and is often ultimately lost. Therefore, be sure to make it a habit to journey and journal immediately afterward.

_____

_____

_____

_____

_____

_____

_____

_____

_____

_____

_____

_____

_____

_____

_____

_____

_____

_____

_____

_____

_____

_____

Exercise 30: To Solve a Problem: Example: How do I know if I should relocate?

The purpose of this exercise is to ask for information and guidance in making the decision to relocate.

Moving to a new location is a time of great stress. Whether it is for a career move, a relationship, or just to make a new start, you never really know if it was the right decision until after it's done. We try to make an informed decision, but it is still a 'leap of faith' about going into the great unknown. So we gather all of the information we can about the place, the climate, the economic situation and the people there. But there is still this nagging doubt about it being the right move for us and our family. It is important to remember that places as well as people have many different aspects to them. Instead of relying solely on the hard data about your prospective home, you can do shamanic journeys to fill in the blanks about the energetic and spiritual aspects as well. Is this a place where you can grow and prosper in all areas of your life?

When you journey for information about a new location, pay attention to the 'feeling' of the place. Does it energize you or does it drain your energy? Are you spiritually uplifted or depressed and lost? Do you relate to the people and the spirits of the land there?

1. Go to a power animal or teacher and ask for information about the nature of the place you are considering going to. Ask to meet the spirits of that place to see if they are welcoming you.

2. Go to a power animal or teacher and ask what you need to know about moving to that place. Is there anything you have forgotten to find out about? Are there any surprises you should be aware of? You can repeat this journey as often as necessary.

After you have defined your intention you can prepare to journey

1. Find a comfortable position so you can relax
2. It helps to have an eye shade to shut out the light

3. Picture your route to the Lower or Upper World clearly in your mind

4. Start the drumming tape or some other percussion tape (rattle, Tibetan bowls, chanting, etc.) (10 min, 20 min or 30 min track)

5. State your intention for the journey in your mind

6. Picture yourself on your path or route to the Lower or Upper World

7. Picture the portal or boundary ahead (whatever you consistently use)

8. State your intention again while approaching the portal or boundary

9. Go into and through the tunnel or boundary; come out into a landscape

10. Look around for your power animal or teacher and again state your intention

11. Go with your power animal or teacher as information is presented about your question

12. When the recall beat sounds, thank your helping spirit and ask him/her to take you back to the boundary

13. Come back via the same route during the double time beat

14. Return to ordinary reality

15. Record the details of your journey immediately so you don't forget them

Interpreting your journey

What did your helping spirit do when you asked the question? Did you receive information telepathically in your mind or did you 'see' something? What was the 'feel' or energy of the information you received? Did your helping spirit take you somewhere and what was the scenario you experienced there? What did you experience through all of your senses?

Journey & Journal

Record your impressions immediately before you forget your experiences. Are you keeping updates in your journal? Remember, the
information you receive when journeying is often like information
you get in a dream—as you return to the beta state of mind much of
the information fades and is often ultimately lost. Therefore, be sure
to make it a habit to journey and journal immediately afterward.

_____

_____

_____

_____

_____

_____

_____

_____

_____

_____

_____

_____

_____

_____

_____

_____

_____

_____

_____

_____

_____

_____

Exercise 31: To Solve a Problem: Example: How do I deal with financial issues?

The purpose of this exercise is to ask for support and guidance in dealing with financial issues.

Trying to cope with financial problems can make you feel extremely helpless and powerless, especially when the general economy is depressed as well. It feels like opportunities are limited and it can be devastating to your self-esteem when rejection is a daily occurrence. In this situation it is really important to enhance and protect your personal power and make the most of the options available to you. Working with your helping spirits on a regular basis will give you access to information and insights on how to maximize your resources and set your priorities. You can also explore the emotional and spiritual aspects of what your finances reflect about you. How does addressing your attitudes and beliefs about prosperity help keep you on track in achieving your financial goals?

When you journey today ask for information about the opportunities available to you. How can you maintain your personal power to take advantage of these opportunities? How can you gain insight into your attitudes and beliefs about prosperity?

1. Ask your power animal or teacher to show you the options available as you deal with conflicting priorities in your finances. How can you best use your strengths and abilities to take advantage of opportunities as they arise?

2. Ask your helping spirits to show you how your attitudes and beliefs about money and prosperity affect your ability to reach your financial goals. How can you revise your belief system to change the energy in your situation?

After you have defined your intention you can prepare to journey

1. Find a comfortable position so you can relax

2. It helps to have an eye shade to shut out the light

3. Picture your route to the Lower or Upper World clearly in your mind

4. Start the drumming tape or some other percussion tape (rattle, Tibetan bowls, chanting, etc.) (10 min, 20 min or 30 min track)

5. State your intention for the journey in your mind

6. Picture yourself on your path or route to the Lower or Upper World

7. Picture the portal or boundary ahead (whatever you consistently use)

8. State your intention again while approaching the portal or boundary

9. Go into and through the tunnel or boundary; come out into a landscape

10. Look around for your power animal or teacher and again state your intention

11. Go with your power animal or teacher as information is presented about your question

12. When the recall beat sounds, thank your helping spirit and ask him/her to take you back to the boundary

13. Come back via the same route during the double time beat

14. Return to ordinary reality

15. Record the details of your journey immediately so you don't forget them

Interpreting your journey

What did your helping spirit do when you asked the question? Did you receive information telepathically in your mind or did you 'see' something? What was the 'feel' or energy of the information you received? Did your helping spirit take you somewhere and what was the scenario you experienced there? What did you experience through all of your senses?

Journey & Journal

Record your impressions immediately before you forget your experiences. Are you keeping updates in your journal? Remember, the information you receive when journeying is often like information you get in a dream—as you return to the beta state of mind much of the information fades and is often ultimately lost. Therefore, be sure to make it a habit to journey and journal immediately afterward.

_____

_____

_____

_____

_____

_____

_____

_____

_____

_____

_____

_____

_____

_____

_____

_____

_____

_____

_____

_____

_____

_____

Exercise 32: To Solve a Problem: Example: How do I retrain for a new career?

The purpose of this exercise is to ask for support and guidance in dealing with retraining for a new career.

Starting over at anything can be stressful because you are dealing with the unknown, but it can be overwhelming when it involves your career. It can be devastating to realize that the work you have been doing for a long time no longer has value and is considered to be out-of-date. So where and how do you begin to find the work that will truly make you feel fulfilled and valued? How do you combine your work with your spiritual mission and still be able to live and pay your bills? Fortunately you have trusted helping spirits that will guide you in matching a career with your life mission. You can use the power of the shamanic journey to explore the path you seek for fulfillment and then embark on the training that will get you there. You can also ask for a power animal or teacher to help you with this specific project. You can ask for their aid throughout the training process, checking to ensure that you are on the right track.

When you journey today ask for information about the opportunities available to you. How can you identify your strengths and abilities in choosing a new career? How can you gain insight into your attitudes and beliefs about starting over?

1. Ask your power animal or teacher to show you the options available as you deal with retraining for a new career. How can you best use your strengths and abilities to take advantage of opportunities as they arise? How can you build on what you have already accomplished to fulfill your life mission?

2. Ask for a power animal or teacher to come and help you with this major change in your life. Continue to journey to them to monitor your progress in meeting your goals and revising your plans.

After you have defined your intention you can prepare to journey

1. Find a comfortable position so you can relax

2. It helps to have an eye shade to shut out the light

3. Picture your route to the Lower or Upper World clearly in your mind

4. Start the drumming tape or some other percussion tape (rattle, Tibetan bowls, chanting, etc.) (10 min, 20 min or 30 min track)

5. State your intention for the journey in your mind

6. Picture yourself on your path or route to the Lower or Upper World

7. Picture the portal or boundary ahead (whatever you consistently use)

8. State your intention again while approaching the portal or boundary

9. Go into and through the tunnel or boundary; come out into a landscape

10. Look around for your power animal or teacher and again state your intention

11. Go with your power animal or teacher as information is presented about your question

12. When the recall beat sounds, thank your helping spirit and ask him/her to take you back to the boundary

13. Come back via the same route during the double time beat

14. Return to ordinary reality

15. Record the details of your journey immediately so you don't forget them

Interpreting your journey

What did your helping spirit do when you asked the question? Did you receive information telepathically in your mind or did you 'see' something? What was the 'feel' or energy of the information you

received? Did your helping spirit take you somewhere and what was the scenario you experienced there? What did you experience through all of your senses?

Journey & Journal

Record your impressions immediately before you forget your experiences. Are you keeping updates in your journal? Remember, the information you receive when journeying is often like information you get in a dream—as you return to the beta state of mind much of the information fades and is often ultimately lost. Therefore, be sure to make it a habit to journey and journal immediately afterward.

_____

_____

_____

_____

_____

_____

_____

_____

_____

_____

_____

_____

_____

_____

_____

_____

_____

_____

_____

_____

Exercise 33: To Solve a Problem:
Example: Starting a Business

The purpose of this exercise is to ask for support and guidance in starting a new business.

You have a great idea and want to chart your own future. Starting your own business can be a minefield of conflicting priorities spread across limited resources. How can you make the right decisions to grow your business and prosper with ethics and integrity? How can you interface appropriately with your customers, giving excellent service and yet charge enough for your products and services? What about the emotional and spiritual aspects of being your own boss? This is where the power of shamanic journeying really helps to set priorities, make the best decisions you can with allocating resources, and maintain your vision with balance and integrity. You can ask for a power animal to be dedicated to your business to give you constant support and guidance in being the best that you can be. Journey, journey and journey some more to stay on track.

This is a long-term project where you will really develop a relationship with your power animal or teacher dedicated to helping your business grow and prosper. You can journey on a regular basis to set the business up the way you want it, and continuously to keep it on track.

1. Ask your power animal or teacher to show you the options and possibilities in setting up your business in the best way to fulfill your mission. How can you imbue your business operations with spiritual integrity?

2. Ask your helping spirits to show you how your talents and abilities fit with your passions to create the best and most fulfilling work for you to pursue. How do you continue to keep your business on the right track?

After you have defined your intention you can prepare to journey

1. Find a comfortable position so you can relax

2. It helps to have an eye shade to shut out the light

3. Picture your route to the Lower or Upper World clearly in your mind

4. Start the drumming tape or some other percussion tape (rattle, Tibetan bowls, chanting, etc.) (10 min, 20 min or 30 min track)

5. State your intention for the journey in your mind

6. Picture yourself on your path or route to the Lower or Upper World

7. Picture the portal or boundary ahead (whatever you consistently use)

8. State your intention again while approaching the portal or boundary

9. Go into and through the tunnel or boundary; come out into a landscape

10. Look around for your power animal or teacher and again state your intention

11. Go with your power animal or teacher as information is presented about your question

12. When the recall beat sounds, thank your helping spirit and ask him/her to take you back to the boundary

13. Come back via the same route during the double time beat

14. Return to ordinary reality

15. Record the details of your journey immediately so you don't forget them

Interpreting your journey

What did your helping spirit do when you asked the question? Did you receive information telepathically in your mind or did you 'see' something? What was the 'feel' or energy of the information you received? Did your helping spirit take you somewhere and what was the scenario you experienced there? What did you experience through all of your senses?

Journey & Journal

Record your impressions immediately before you forget your experiences. Are you keeping updates in your journal? Remember, the information you receive when journeying is often like information you get in a dream—as you return to the beta state of mind much of the information fades and is often ultimately lost. Therefore, be sure to make it a habit to journey and journal immediately afterward.

_____

_____

_____

_____

_____

_____

_____

_____

_____

_____

_____

_____

_____

_____

_____

_____

_____

_____

_____

_____

_____

_____

_____

_____

Exercise 34: To Solve a Problem: Example: Is there more to my health challenge than just physical issues?

The purpose of this exercise is to ask for information and guidance in restoring my state of perfect health.

We all have many aspects to our complete being, including physical, emotional, mental, spiritual and energetic. If any of these aspects is out of balance, it affects the others. Chronic physical health challenges are often improved by addressing emotional and spiritual issues that may have been undetected for years. When you have tried many different protocols for the same condition with few positive results, it is time to consider other factors that may be affecting your ability to heal. There may be an underlying belief system, a past traumatic experience, or a family 'rule' that has been passed from generation to generation. Awareness of this influence is the first step towards healing it. It may take several iterations to completely restore balance and harmony, so don't give up until you feel that all issues have been addressed.

You can ask your helping spirits for a healing at any time. They are happy to oblige since healing the individual helps to restore balance and harmony to the whole. They can also give you valuable information about what caused the health condition in the first place, even tracing it back through ancestral generations.

1. Go to a power animal or teacher and ask for a healing. You can also ask if there is anything you can do to accelerate your return to a healthy state.

2. Go to a power animal or teacher and ask if there is an emotional or spiritual issue affecting your ability to heal. When did this issue start and how has it influenced your health? What do you need to do to address this issue? Can you do it yourself or do you need to consult a professional?

After you have defined your intention you can prepare to journey

1. Find a comfortable position so you can relax

2. It helps to have an eye shade to shut out the light

3. Picture your route to the Lower or Upper World clearly in your mind

4. Start the drumming tape or some other percussion tape (rattle, Tibetan bowls, chanting, etc.) (10 min, 20 min or 30 min track)

5. State your intention for the journey in your mind

6. Picture yourself on your path or route to the Lower or Upper World

7. Picture the portal or boundary ahead (whatever you consistently use)

8. State your intention again while approaching the portal or boundary

9. Go into and through the tunnel or boundary; come out into a landscape

10. Look around for your power animal or teacher and again state your intention

11. Go with your power animal or teacher as information is presented about your question

12. When the recall beat sounds, thank your helping spirit and ask him/her to take you back to the boundary

13. Come back via the same route during the double time beat

14. Return to ordinary reality

15. Record the details of your journey immediately so you don't forget them

Interpreting your journey

What did your helping spirit do when you asked the question? Did you receive information telepathically in your mind or did you 'see' something? What was the 'feel' or energy of the information you received? Did your helping spirit take you somewhere and what was the scenario you experienced there? What did you experience through all of your senses?

Journey & Journal

Record your impressions immediately before you forget your experiences. Are you keeping updates in your journal? Remember, the information you receive when journeying is often like information you get in a dream—as you return to the beta state of mind much of the information fades and is often ultimately lost. Therefore, be sure to make it a habit to journey and journal immediately afterward.

_____

_____

_____

_____

_____

_____

_____

_____

_____

_____

_____

_____

_____

_____

_____

_____

_____

_____

_____

_____

_____

Exercise 35: To Solve a Problem: Example: Coping With Depression

The purpose of this exercise is to ask for support and guidance in healing anxiety and depression.

Anxiety attacks and depression are just about the exact opposite of feeling empowered and in control. The power of the shamanic journey does not take the place of medical or psychiatric therapies. Instead it works best when used in conjunction with professional help. What journeying CAN do is help you to know that you are not alone, that you have friends in the spirit realm that are willing to support and guide you as you struggle to regain control of your life. It is very comforting to know that you have a power animal that is dedicated to helping you find health and well-being. That power animal will bring you exactly the strengths and abilities you need to define and cope with the underlying issues causing the disharmony and imbalance. Restoring that balance and harmony is what makes it possible to achieve happiness and fulfillment. Shamanism addresses the spiritual aspects of all dis-ease by helping us find ourselves, accept every part of ourselves, and it presents practical ways for us to improve ourselves.

If you feel fragile today, simply ask your power animal or teacher for a healing during the journey. It is not necessary for you to always ask for information or guidance. Restoring your life force and vitality may have to come first.

1. Ask your power animal or teacher to give you a healing aimed at restoring your health and well-being. Ask to be shown where and why your energy is depleted and how to replenish it.

2. Ask your helping spirits to give you practical suggestions to get your life back on track. What are the things you can do for yourself to enhance the work you are doing with professional therapies?

After you have defined your intention you can prepare to journey

1. Find a comfortable position so you can relax
2. It helps to have an eye shade to shut out the light
3. Picture your route to the Lower or Upper World clearly in your mind
4. Start the drumming tape or some other percussion tape (rattle, Tibetan bowls, chanting, etc.) (10 min, 20 min or 30 min track)
5. State your intention for the journey in your mind
6. Picture yourself on your path or route to the Lower or Upper World
7. Picture the portal or boundary ahead (whatever you consistently use)
8. State your intention again while approaching the portal or boundary
9. Go into and through the tunnel or boundary; come out into a landscape
10. Look around for your power animal or teacher and again state your intention
11. Go with your power animal or teacher as information is presented about your question
12. When the recall beat sounds, thank your helping spirit and ask him/her to take you back to the boundary
13. Come back via the same route during the double time beat
14. Return to ordinary reality
15. Record the details of your journey immediately so you don't forget them

Interpreting your journey

What did your helping spirit do when you asked the question? Did you receive information telepathically in your mind or did you 'see' something? What was the 'feel' or energy of the information you

received? Did your helping spirit take you somewhere and what was the scenario you experienced there? What did you experience through all of your senses?

Journey & Journal

Record your impressions immediately before you forget your experiences. Are you keeping updates in your journal? Remember, the information you receive when journeying is often like information you get in a dream—as you return to the beta state of mind much of the information fades and is often ultimately lost. Therefore, be sure to make it a habit to journey and journal immediately afterward.

_____

_____

_____

_____

_____

_____

_____

_____

_____

_____

_____

_____

_____

_____

_____

_____

_____

_____

_____

_____

_____

_____

Exercise 36: To Solve a Problem: Example: Coping with Excess Weight

The purpose of this exercise is to ask for support and guidance in achieving your perfect healthy weight.

There can be many reasons for being overweight. Carrying excess weight can be a symptom of carrying emotional and/or spiritual baggage. It can also be the result of a physical medical condition or just plain not eating right. Whatever the reason, it can affect our self-esteem, our self-image and our health. For many, this is truly a life-long struggle and we need all the help and support we can get. The best thing about working with your helping spirits is that they don't judge you. If you are willing to ask for their support and guidance, they are willing to give you healing and practical advice. The best part is that they can help you get to the underlying cause(s) of why this condition manifested in the first place. Once you understand the issues and physical, emotional or spiritual imbalances, you can ask for healings in your journeys. You can also ask for practical ways to address the issues involved. Awareness promotes understanding, which leads to restoring your perfect blueprint for your healthy weight.

If you feel fragile today, simply ask your power animal or teacher for a healing during the journey. It is not necessary for you to always ask for information or guidance. Restoring your life force and vitality may have to come first.

1. Ask your power animal or teacher to give you a healing aimed at restoring your health and well-being. Ask to be shown where and why your energy is depleted and how to replenish it. What does this have to do with carrying excess weight?

2. Ask your helping spirits to give you practical suggestions to get control of your life and control of your diet. What are the things you can do for yourself to understand and deal with the underlying issues involved?

After you have defined your intention you can prepare to journey

1. Find a comfortable position so you can relax

2. It helps to have an eye shade to shut out the light

3. Picture your route to the Lower or Upper World clearly in your mind

4. Start the drumming tape or some other percussion tape (rattle, Tibetan bowls, chanting, etc.) (10 min, 20 min or 30 min track)

5. State your intention for the journey in your mind

6. Picture yourself on your path or route to the Lower or Upper World

7. Picture the portal or boundary ahead (whatever you consistently use)

8. State your intention again while approaching the portal or boundary

9. Go into and through the tunnel or boundary; come out into a landscape

10. Look around for your power animal or teacher and again state your intention

11. Go with your power animal or teacher as information is presented about your question

12. When the recall beat sounds, thank your helping spirit and ask him/her to take you back to the boundary

13. Come back via the same route during the double time beat

14. Return to ordinary reality

15. Record the details of your journey immediately so you don't forget them

Interpreting your journey

What did your helping spirit do when you asked the question? Did you receive information telepathically in your mind or did you 'see' something? What was the 'feel' or energy of the information you

received? Did your helping spirit take you somewhere and what was the scenario you experienced there? What did you experience through all of your senses?

Journey & Journal

Record your impressions immediately before you forget your experiences. Are you keeping updates in your journal? Remember, the information you receive when journeying is often like information you get in a dream—as you return to the beta state of mind much of the information fades and is often ultimately lost. Therefore, be sure to make it a habit to journey and journal immediately afterward.

_____

_____

_____

_____

_____

_____

_____

_____

_____

_____

_____

_____

_____

_____

_____

_____

_____

_____

_____

_____

_____

_____

Exercise 37: To Solve a Problem: Example: Coping with Burn-Out

The purpose of this exercise is to ask for support and guidance in maintaining commitment without burning out.

Being dedicated and committed to your work is a good thing, but not at the price of your health and sanity. The key to achieving happiness, fulfillment and serenity is balance between work, play and time for self. This is easy to say but often difficult to manifest as we all struggle with too much to do and not enough time to do it. I often say that I have trouble getting done the things I HAVE to do, much less the things I SHOULD do. It seems that I never get to the things I WANT to do. It is even more difficult when we are in a service or healing profession. The temptation is to give and give until we are depleted in body, mind and spirit. By using the power of shamanic journeying, you can work with your helping spirits to restore your energy and your commitment to your work. The spirits are eager to assist you in helping others to heal and thrive. They will also give you practical advice in how to maintain boundaries and limits so that you don't get burned out in the first place.

If you feel fragile today, simply ask your power animal or teacher for a healing during the journey. It is not necessary for you to always ask for information or guidance. Restoring your life force and vitality may have to come first.

1. Ask your power animal or teacher to give you a healing aimed at restoring your health and well-being. Ask to be shown where and why your energy is depleted and how to replenish it. How can you avoid overdoing it in the future?

2. Ask your helping spirits to give you practical suggestions to get control of your life and control of your time. What are the things you can do for yourself to understand and deal with the underlying issues involved? What gives you joy and how can you access more of that?

After you have defined your intention you can prepare to journey

1. Find a comfortable position so you can relax

2. It helps to have an eye shade to shut out the light

3. Picture your route to the Lower or Upper World clearly in your mind

4. Start the drumming tape or some other percussion tape (rattle, Tibetan bowls, chanting, etc.) (10 min, 20 min or 30 min track)

5. State your intention for the journey in your mind

6. Picture yourself on your path or route to the Lower or Upper World

7. Picture the portal or boundary ahead (whatever you consistently use)

8. State your intention again while approaching the portal or boundary

9. Go into and through the tunnel or boundary; come out into a landscape

10. Look around for your power animal or teacher and again state your intention

11. Go with your power animal or teacher as information is presented about your question

12. When the recall beat sounds, thank your helping spirit and ask him/her to take you back to the boundary

13. Come back via the same route during the double time beat

14. Return to ordinary reality

15. Record the details of your journey immediately so you don't forget them

Interpreting your journey

What did your helping spirit do when you asked the question? Did you receive information telepathically in your mind or did you 'see' something? What was the 'feel' or energy of the information you

received? Did your helping spirit take you somewhere and what was the scenario you experienced there? What did you experience through all of your senses?

Journey & Journal

Record your impressions immediately before you forget your experiences. Are you keeping updates in your journal? Remember, the information you receive when journeying is often like information you get in a dream—as you return to the beta state of mind much of the information fades and is often ultimately lost. Therefore, be sure to make it a habit to journey and journal immediately afterward.

_____

_____

_____

_____

_____

_____

_____

_____

_____

_____

_____

_____

_____

_____

_____

_____

_____

_____

_____

Exercise 38: To Solve a Problem: Example: Coping with Serious Illness

The purpose of this exercise is to ask for support and guidance in dealing with serious illness.

It has been proven that in dealing with serious illness, your attitude towards not just coping but healing has a great effect on the success of whatever protocol you are on. It is also true that all disease is a combination of physical, emotional, mental and spiritual imbalance and disharmony. Since we are all unique individuals, it is imperative that you find the right treatment protocol that will give you maximum opportunities to heal. This may include conventional and alternative modalities, as well as methods to achieve emotional and spiritual peace and tranquility. By using the power of the shamanic journey, you can investigate what caused the imbalance in the first place, whether it is genetic, emotional, or a combination of mental beliefs and lifestyle practices. You can ask your helping spirits for spiritual healing to restore harmony and for guidance on which modalities are best for you. Most of all, you will receive the support that you need to move into being proactive rather than reactive, no matter what the eventual outcome is. In shamanism, death is also a form of healing, not a process to be feared. Your helping spirits will be there to support and guide you through this difficult time.

If you feel fragile today, simply ask your power animal or teacher for a healing during the journey. It is not necessary for you to always ask for information or guidance. Restoring your life force and vitality may have to come first.

1. Ask your power animal or teacher to give you a healing aimed at restoring your health and well-being. Ask to be shown where and why your energy is depleted and how to replenish it. How can you achieve peace and serenity?

2. Ask your helping spirits to give you practical suggestions to get control of your life and health. What are the things you can do for yourself to understand and deal with the underlying issues involved? What practices give you the greatest opportunities to heal?

After you have defined your intention you can prepare to journey

1. Find a comfortable position so you can relax

2. It helps to have an eye shade to shut out the light

3. Picture your route to the Lower or Upper World clearly in your mind

4. Start the drumming tape or some other percussion tape (rattle, Tibetan bowls, chanting, etc.) (10 min, 20 min or 30 min track)

5. State your intention for the journey in your mind

6. Picture yourself on your path or route to the Lower or Upper World

7. Picture the portal or boundary ahead (whatever you consistently use)

8. State your intention again while approaching the portal or boundary

9. Go into and through the tunnel or boundary; come out into a landscape

10. Look around for your power animal or teacher and again state your intention

11. Go with your power animal or teacher as information is presented about your question

12. When the recall beat sounds, thank your helping spirit and ask him/her to take you back to the boundary

13. Come back via the same route during the double time beat

14. Return to ordinary reality

15. Record the details of your journey immediately so you don't forget them

Interpreting your journey

What did your helping spirit do when you asked the question? Did you receive information telepathically in your mind or did you 'see' something? What was the 'feel' or energy of the information you

received? Did your helping spirit take you somewhere and what was the scenario you experienced there? What did you experience through all of your senses?

Journey & Journal

Record your impressions immediately before you forget your experiences. Are you keeping updates in your journal? Remember, the information you receive when journeying is often like information you get in a dream—as you return to the beta state of mind much of the information fades and is often ultimately lost. Therefore, be sure to make it a habit to journey and journal immediately afterward.

_____

_____

_____

_____

_____

_____

_____

_____

_____

_____

_____

_____

_____

_____

_____

_____

_____

_____

_____

_____

_____

_____

Exercise 39: To Solve a Problem: Example:
How do I know what my life mission is?

The purpose of this exercise is to ask for information and guidance in finding what I am here to do.

We know that we are here to live and learn, to work and play, to create and procreate. But there comes a time in most everyone's life when we wonder if that is really all there is to it. Most of us start with a vague feeling that there should be more, that we should be doing more. The problem is that we don't have a clue what that means or what to do about it. How do you find out what your purpose is? How do you know that your life reflects your true mission? Do you have a mission? And is it totally different than what you are doing? These are the thoughts and feelings that send people searching for their own form of spirituality, for a meaning for their existence. Some find it in their religious practice and some search other avenues. Shamanism does not conflict with any religious practice. Instead it helps you determine that you are on the right path in expressing your own spirituality. This is known as 'soul remembering,' discovering and remembering your purpose in coming here to this life.

When you journey for information about your life purpose, it is important to have an open mind, to explore all possibilities. Are you drawn to certain places or activities? What feels very 'natural' to you?

1. Go to a power animal or teacher and ask for signs or examples that you are following the right path to accomplish your mission. Ask to explore what spirituality means to you and how you express it.

2. Go to a power animal or teacher and ask for opportunities to learn about different ways to express spirituality. Ask how such opportunities have been presented to you in the past. Ask for help in defining your purpose or mission in this lifetime.

After you have defined your intention you can prepare to journey

1. Find a comfortable position so you can relax

2. It helps to have an eye shade to shut out the light

3. Picture your route to the Lower or Upper World clearly in your mind

4. Start the drumming tape or some other percussion tape (rattle, Tibetan bowls, chanting, etc.) (10 min, 20 min or 30 min track)

5. State your intention for the journey in your mind

6. Picture yourself on your path or route to the Lower or Upper World

7. Picture the portal or boundary ahead (whatever you consistently use)

8. State your intention again while approaching the portal or boundary

9. Go into and through the tunnel or boundary; come out into a landscape

10. Look around for your power animal or teacher and again state your intention

11. Go with your power animal or teacher as information is presented about your question

12. When the recall beat sounds, thank your helping spirit and ask him/her to take you back to the boundary

13. Come back via the same route during the double time beat

14. Return to ordinary reality

15. Record the details of your journey immediately so you don't forget them

Interpreting your journey

What did your helping spirit do when you asked the question? Did you receive information telepathically in your mind or did you 'see' something? What was the 'feel' or energy of the information you

received? Did your helping spirit take you somewhere and what was the scenario you experienced there? What did you experience through all of your senses?

Journey & Journal

Record your impressions immediately before you forget your experiences. Are you keeping updates in your journal? Remember, the information you receive when journeying is often like information you get in a dream—as you return to the beta state of mind much of the information fades and is often ultimately lost. Therefore, be sure to make it a habit to journey and journal immediately afterward.

_____

_____

_____

_____

_____

_____

_____

_____

_____

_____

_____

_____

_____

_____

_____

_____

_____

_____

_____

_____

RESOURCES

Websites

www.shamanicteachers.com
www.shamanicstudies.org
www.shamansociety.org
www.shamanportal.org
www.web-us.com/primitivebeats.htm
www.lilytherese.com/POWER1.HTM
www.animalspirits.com/index1.html
www.shamanism.org
www.shamanlinks.net
www.allaboutspirituality.org/shamanism.htm

Associations

The Foundation for Shamanic Studies. www.samanicstudies.org
Society for Shamanic Practitioners. www.shamansociety.org
International Shaman Society. http://www.freewebs.com/eclear/
   intshamansociety.htm
Dance of the Deer Foundation. http://danceofthedeer.com
Society for Shamanic Practitioners, UK, http://www.shamanicwar-
   rior.com

BIBLIOGRAPHY

Cowan, Tom. *Shamanism as a Spiritual Practice for Daily Life.* Freedom: The Crossing Press, 1996.

Harner, Michael. *The Way of the Shaman.* San Francisco: HarperSanFrancisco, 1990.

Heaven, Ross and Howard G. Charing. *Plant Spirit Shamanism.* Rochester: Destiny Books, 2006.

Ingerman, Sandra. *Shamanic Journeying: A Beginner's Guide.* Boulder: Sounds True, 2004.

Meadows, Kenneth. *Shamanic Spirit: A Practical Guide to Personal Fulfillment.* Rochester: Bear & Co., 2004.

Pogacnik, Marko. *Nature Spirits & Elemental Beings.* Tallahassee: Findhorn Press, 1995.

Scott, Gini Graham. *The Complete Idiot's Guide to Shamanism.* Indianapolis: Alpha Books, 2002.

Resources that provide additional information about power animals and magical creatures:

Andrews, Ted. *Animal-Speak.* St. Paul: Llewellyn Publications, 1995.

Andrews, Ted. *Animal-Wise.* Jackson: Dragonhawk Publishing, 1999.

Farmer, Steven D. *Animal Spirit Guides.* Carlsbad: Hay House, Inc, 2006.

Matthews, John & Caitlin. *The Element Encyclopedia of Magical Creatures.* Harper Element, 2005.

Sams, Jamie and David Carson. *Medicine Cards: the discovery of power through the ways of animals.* St. Martin's Press, 1999.